AI 101: A Beginner's Guide to Artificial Intelligence

Table of Contents:

CHAPTER 1

Introduction to Artificial Intelligence

AI 101: A Beginner's Guide to Artificial Intelligence is designed to provide you with a comprehensive understanding of artificial intelligence from its fundamental concepts to its practical applications. Whether you are a student, professional, or simply curious about the field of AI, this ebook will serve as your starting point in exploring the exciting world of AI.

Throughout this ebook, we will explore various topics, including the types of AI, machine learning, deep learning, AI development processes, and ethical considerations in AI. We will also delve into real-world applications of AI and discuss its future implications.

By the end of this guide, you will have gained a solid foundation in AI concepts, enabling you to explore advanced topics and pursue further learning opportunities in this rapidly evolving field.

Note: This ebook is intended for beginners and assumes no prior knowledge of AI. However, a basic understanding of programming concepts will be beneficial in understanding certain sections.

1.1 What is Artificial Intelligence?

Artificial Intelligence (AI) is a branch of computer science that focuses on creating intelligent machines that can perform tasks that typically require human intelligence. AI aims to develop systems capable of perceiving, reasoning, learning, and making decisions in a way that mimics human intelligence.

At its core, AI involves the development of algorithms and models that enable machines to process and interpret data, learn from experience, and adapt to new information. AI systems can analyze vast amounts of data, identify patterns, make predictions, and automate complex tasks with efficiency and accuracy.

AI can be broadly categorized into two types: Narrow AI and General AI. Narrow AI, also known as Weak AI, is designed to perform specific tasks within a defined domain, such as image recognition, language translation, or speech synthesis. General AI, also referred to as Strong AI or AGI (Artificial General Intelligence), aims to exhibit the same level of intelligence and versatility as a human being, capable of understanding and performing any intellectual task.

AI techniques often rely on subfields like machine learning, deep learning, and reinforcement learning. Machine learning involves training models to recognize patterns and make predictions based on data. Deep learning, a subset of machine learning, utilizes artificial neural networks with multiple layers to process complex data and extract high-level representations. Reinforcement learning focuses on training AI agents to learn through trial-and-error interactions with an environment.

AI has a wide range of applications across various industries, including healthcare, finance, transportation, gaming, customer service, and more. It has the potential to revolutionize the way we live, work, and interact with technology.

In summary, AI is a field of study and practice that aims to create intelligent machines capable of performing tasks that traditionally require human intelligence. By leveraging algorithms, models, and data, AI systems can process information, learn from experience, and make decisions, leading to improved efficiency, accuracy, and problem-solving capabilities.

1.2 The History of Artificial Intelligence

The history of Artificial Intelligence (AI) dates back to ancient times, where philosophers and thinkers contemplated the concept of creating machines that could mimic human intelligence. However, the modern development of AI as a scientific discipline began in the mid-20th century. Let's explore some key milestones and breakthroughs in the history of AI:

1. Dartmouth Conference (1956): Considered the birth of AI, the Dartmouth Conference brought together a group of scientists who coined the term "Artificial Intelligence." The participants aimed to explore how machines could simulate human intelligence and solve complex problems.

2. Early AI Programs: In the late 1950s and early 1960s, researchers developed several foundational AI programs. Notable examples include the Logic Theorist, a program that could prove mathematical theorems, and the General Problem Solver, designed to solve a wide range of problems using a set of rules.

3. Expert Systems (1960s-1970s): Expert systems were developed to capture human expertise in specific domains. These rule-based systems used knowledge representation techniques to provide expert-level advice and solve complex problems. Examples include DENDRAL, an expert system for chemical analysis, and MYCIN, which diagnosed bacterial infections.

4. The AI Winter (1970s-1980s): Progress in AI faced challenges and setbacks during this period, known as the "AI Winter." High expectations and the inability to fulfill them led to reduced funding and skepticism surrounding AI's capabilities. However, research continued in specialized areas.

5. Machine Learning and Neural Networks: In the 1980s and 1990s, there was a resurgence of interest in AI, particularly in the field of machine learning. Researchers focused on developing algorithms that could learn from data and improve their performance. Neural networks, inspired by the structure of the human brain, gained attention for their ability to model complex patterns.

6. Big Data and Deep Learning: With the advent of the internet and the explosion of data in the early 2000s, AI witnessed significant

advancements. Deep learning, enabled by the availability of large datasets and powerful computing resources, revolutionized AI by achieving remarkable results in areas like computer vision and natural language processing.

7. AI in the 21st Century: AI has experienced exponential growth and integration into various aspects of our lives in recent years. Breakthroughs in AI, such as self-driving cars, virtual assistants, and sophisticated recommendation systems, have transformed industries and daily interactions. AI has also played a crucial role in areas like healthcare diagnostics, fraud detection, and personalized marketing.

Today, AI continues to evolve rapidly, with ongoing research and development in areas like explainable AI, reinforcement learning, and ethical considerations. As technology advances and AI becomes more integrated into society, the future holds exciting possibilities for AI-driven innovations and solutions.

In summary, the history of AI spans several decades, from the initial conceptualization of intelligent machines to the development of sophisticated algorithms and applications. While AI has faced periods of skepticism, it has made significant progress, and its impact on various industries and everyday life continues to grow.

1.3 Real-World Applications of Artificial Intelligence

Artificial Intelligence (AI) has found diverse applications across a wide range of industries, revolutionizing how tasks are performed, improving efficiency, and enabling new possibilities. Let's explore some notable real-world applications of AI:

1. Healthcare: AI has made significant contributions to the healthcare industry. It is being used for disease diagnosis, medical image analysis, drug discovery, and personalized medicine.

AI-powered systems can analyze medical records, images, and genetic data to assist doctors in making accurate diagnoses and treatment plans. It also plays a role in monitoring patient health, predicting disease outbreaks, and managing healthcare resources efficiently.

2. Finance: AI has transformed the finance sector by automating processes, enhancing fraud detection, and improving customer service. Machine learning algorithms can analyze vast amounts of financial data, identify patterns, and make predictions for investment strategies. AI-powered chatbots provide personalized customer support and assist in managing finances. Additionally, AI algorithms help in detecting fraudulent transactions and mitigating risks in real-time.

3. Transportation: AI has revolutionized transportation systems by enabling autonomous vehicles and optimizing traffic management. Self-driving cars, powered by AI technologies like computer vision and machine learning, are being developed to improve road safety and efficiency. AI is also used for route optimization, fleet management, and predictive maintenance of vehicles. Additionally, AI-based algorithms help in managing traffic flow and reducing congestion in urban areas.

4. Retail and E-commerce: AI is transforming the retail and e-commerce landscape through personalized recommendations, demand forecasting, and inventory management. AI algorithms analyze customer data, browsing patterns, and purchase history to provide personalized product recommendations. Chatbots powered by AI offer customer support and assistance in navigating online stores. AI-driven demand forecasting helps retailers optimize their inventory and supply chain operations.

5. Natural Language Processing (NLP): NLP is a field of AI that focuses on the interaction between computers and human language. It enables applications like virtual assistants (e.g., Siri, Alexa) that can understand and respond to voice commands. NLP also powers language translation services, sentiment analysis in social media, and chatbots that can engage in natural language conversations.

6. Manufacturing and Robotics: AI is transforming the manufacturing industry by optimizing production processes, predictive maintenance, and quality control. AI-powered robots and automation systems are being used to perform repetitive tasks with precision and efficiency. Machine learning algorithms analyze sensor data to detect anomalies and predict maintenance needs, reducing downtime and improving productivity.

7. Energy and Sustainability: AI plays a role in energy management and sustainability initiatives. AI algorithms optimize energy consumption in buildings, predict energy demand, and facilitate smart grid management. AI also contributes to environmental monitoring, precision agriculture, and optimizing resource allocation in renewable energy systems.

8. Entertainment and Gaming: AI has had a significant impact on the entertainment industry, from personalized content recommendations on streaming platforms to AI-generated music and artwork. AI algorithms enhance gaming experiences by powering intelligent non-player characters (NPCs), realistic simulations, and adaptive gameplay.

These are just a few examples of the real-world applications of AI. The potential of AI is vast, and its impact continues to grow across industries, enabling innovation, automation, and improved decision-making processes. As technology advances, AI is expected to further revolutionize various sectors and create new opportunities.

CHAPTER 2

Types of Artificial Intelligence

2.1 Narrow AI vs. General AI

Artificial Intelligence (AI) can be broadly classified into two categories: Narrow AI (also known as Weak AI) and General AI (also known as Strong AI or Artificial General Intelligence). Let's explore the differences between these two types:

Narrow AI:

Narrow AI refers to AI systems that are designed to perform specific tasks within a limited domain. These systems excel at a particular task or set of tasks but lack the ability to generalize their intelligence to other domains or perform tasks beyond their specific programming. Examples of narrow AI include voice assistants like Siri or Alexa, image recognition systems, recommendation engines, and autonomous vehicles.

Characteristics of Narrow AI:

1. Specialized: Narrow AI systems are built to excel in specific tasks, such as speech recognition, image classification, or playing chess.

2. Domain-Specific: They operate within a well-defined domain and are optimized for specific use cases.

3. Limited Scope: Narrow AI lacks the ability to transfer knowledge or skills to different domains or tasks.
4. Data-Driven: Narrow AI relies on large amounts of training data to learn patterns and make predictions.

5. Predefined Rules: These AI systems follow predefined rules and algorithms to accomplish their tasks.

General AI:

General AI, on the other hand, refers to AI systems that possess the ability to understand, learn, and apply intelligence across a wide range of tasks and domains. General AI aims to replicate human-like intelligence, allowing machines to reason, learn, and adapt in a manner similar to human beings. A true general AI system would have the capability to understand diverse concepts, learn from experience, and perform any intellectual task that a human can.

Characteristics of General AI:

1. Versatile: General AI systems are designed to exhibit intelligence and problem-solving abilities across various domains.

2. Transferable Skills: They can transfer knowledge and skills from one domain to another, enabling adaptation to new tasks.

3. Contextual Understanding: General AI can understand and interpret information in a contextual manner, similar to human comprehension.

4. Learning and Reasoning: These systems can learn from experience, reason, make decisions, and continuously improve their performance.

5. Self-Awareness: General AI systems possess self-awareness and consciousness, understanding their own existence and goals.

It is essential to note that while narrow AI has made significant progress and has practical applications in various fields, general AI remains an ongoing area of research and development. Creating a system with the level of cognitive capabilities and adaptability seen in humans is a complex challenge that requires advancements in several areas of AI.

In summary, narrow AI refers to AI systems designed for specific tasks within a limited domain, while general AI represents the pursuit of AI systems that possess human-like intelligence and can perform a wide range of tasks across different domains. While narrow AI is prevalent and practical today, general AI remains an ambitious goal that continues to drive AI research and development.

2.2 Machine Learning

Machine Learning (ML) is a subfield of Artificial Intelligence (AI) that focuses on the development of algorithms and models that enable computers to learn and make predictions or decisions without being explicitly programmed. It allows machines to automatically learn from data, identify patterns, and improve their performance over time. Machine Learning has become a powerful tool in solving complex problems and making data-driven decisions. Let's explore the key concepts and types of Machine Learning:

Key Concepts in Machine Learning:

1. Data: Machine Learning algorithms rely on data as their primary source of information. High-quality and relevant data is crucial for training models and making accurate predictions.

2. Features: Features are the measurable characteristics or attributes of the data that ML algorithms use to make predictions. Effective feature selection and engineering are vital for the performance of ML models.

3. Training: In the training phase, ML algorithms learn from labeled or unlabeled data to identify patterns and relationships. They adjust their internal parameters based on the provided examples to improve their accuracy.

4. Models: Machine Learning models are mathematical representations created by algorithms. They capture patterns and relationships in the training data and use them to make predictions or decisions.

5. Evaluation: After training, ML models need to be evaluated on unseen data to assess their performance. Evaluation metrics such as accuracy, precision, recall, and F1 score help measure the model's effectiveness.

6. Generalization: ML models aim to generalize their knowledge to unseen data. They should perform well on new, unseen examples to demonstrate their ability to understand underlying patterns beyond the training set.

Types of Machine Learning:

1. Superrvised Learning: Supervised Learning involves training ML models with labeled data, where each example has an associated target or output. The models learn to map input features to the correct output by minimizing the error between predicted and true values. Supervised Learning is used for tasks like classification (assigning labels to inputs) and regression (predicting continuous values).

2. Unsupervised Learning: Unsupervised Learning involves training ML models with unlabeled data, where the model must identify inherent patterns or structures on its own. It is used for tasks such as clustering (grouping similar data points), dimensionality reduction (reducing the number of features), and anomaly detection (identifying abnormal data points).

3. Semi-Supervised Learning: Semi-Supervised Learning is a combination of supervised and unsupervised learning. It uses a small amount of labeled data and a larger amount of unlabeled data for training. It leverages the relationships and patterns in both labeled and unlabeled data to improve the model's performance.

4. Reinforcement Learning: Reinforcement Learning involves training agents to learn from interactions with an environment. The agent receives feedback in the form of rewards or penalties based on its actions, and its goal is to maximize cumulative rewards over time. Reinforcement Learning is used in applications like game playing, robotics, and autonomous systems.

Machine Learning has become a fundamental technique in various domains, including healthcare, finance, marketing, image and speech recognition, recommendation systems, and natural language processing. Its ability to analyze large datasets, discover patterns, and make predictions has significantly advanced problem-solving and decision-making capabilities.

In summary, Machine Learning is a subfield of AI that enables computers to learn from data and make predictions or decisions without explicit programming. Through training on labeled or unlabeled data, ML models identify patterns and relationships to make accurate predictions. Supervised, unsupervised, semi-supervised, and reinforcement learning are the main types of Machine Learning, each suited for specific tasks and data characteristics.

2.3 Deep Learning

Deep Learning is a subfield of Machine Learning that focuses on the development and application of artificial neural networks with multiple layers, known as deep neural networks. Deep Learning algorithms aim to learn hierarchical representations of data by progressively extracting higher-level features from raw input. It has gained significant attention and revolutionized various domains, including computer vision, natural language processing, and speech recognition. Let's explore the key concepts and components of Deep Learning:

Key Concepts in Deep Learning:

1. Neural Networks: Neural networks are computational models inspired by the structure and functioning of the human brain. They consist of interconnected nodes, called neurons, organized in layers. Each neuron receives input, applies a mathematical operation, and produces an output.

2. Deep Neural Networks: Deep Neural Networks, also known as deep nets or deep learning models, are neural networks with multiple hidden layers between the input and output layers. Deep networks can learn complex representations by capturing intricate patterns and dependencies in data.

3. Activation Functions: Activation functions introduce non-linearity to neural networks, enabling them to model complex relationships in data. Popular activation functions include sigmoid, hyperbolic tangent (tanh), and rectified linear unit (ReLU).

4. Backpropagation: Backpropagation is a key algorithm used to train deep neural networks. It calculates the gradient of the loss function with respect to the network's parameters and adjusts the weights of the connections through an iterative optimization process.

5. Convolutional Neural Networks (CNNs): CNNs are a type of deep neural network specifically designed for processing grid-like data,

such as images. They utilize convolutional layers to automatically learn hierarchical representations of visual features, enabling tasks like image classification, object detection, and image generation.

6. Recurrent Neural Networks (RNNs): RNNs are a type of deep neural network that can process sequential data, such as time series or natural language. They maintain internal memory to capture dependencies and temporal information across different time steps, making them suitable for tasks like language modeling, machine translation, and speech recognition.

7. Transfer Learning: Transfer Learning is a technique in Deep Learning where knowledge learned from one task or domain is transferred and applied to another related task or domain. It allows models trained on large datasets and complex tasks to be leveraged for new tasks with limited data.

Deep Learning has achieved remarkable results in various applications. It has revolutionized computer vision with state-of-the-art object recognition and image segmentation. In natural language processing, deep learning models have significantly improved machine translation, sentiment analysis, and text generation. Deep Learning has also played a crucial role in speech recognition, recommender systems, and autonomous vehicles.

Deep Learning models require substantial computational resources and large amounts of labeled data to train effectively. Advances in hardware acceleration, such as Graphics Processing Units (GPUs) and specialized chips like Tensor Processing Units (TPUs), have accelerated the training and inference of deep networks.

In summary, Deep Learning is a subfield of Machine Learning that focuses on training deep neural networks with multiple layers to learn hierarchical representations of data. Convolutional Neural Networks (CNNs) excel in computer vision tasks, while Recurrent Neural Networks

(RNNs) are powerful for sequential data. Deep Learning has made significant contributions to various domains and continues to drive advancements in AI research and applications.

2.4 Reinforcement Learning

Reinforcement Learning (RL) is a subfield of Machine Learning that focuses on training agents to make a sequence of decisions in an environment to maximize cumulative rewards. RL is inspired by the way humans and animals learn through trial and error interactions with their surroundings. It has been successfully applied to various complex tasks, such as game playing, robotics, autonomous systems, and recommendation systems. Let's explore the key concepts and components of Reinforcement Learning:

Key Concepts in Reinforcement Learning:

1. Agent: An agent is the learner or decision-maker that interacts with an environment. It takes actions based on its current state and receives feedback in the form of rewards or penalties from the environment.

2. Environment: The environment is the external context with which the agent interacts. It provides the agent with the current state, receives actions from the agent, and updates the state based on those actions.

3. State: The state represents the current condition or observation of the environment. It contains all the relevant information necessary for the agent to make decisions.

4. Action: An action is a specific move or decision that the agent takes in a particular state. Actions can have

immediate consequences, affecting the subsequent state and the rewards received.

5. Reward: The reward is a scalar feedback signal that indicates the desirability or quality of the agent's action in a given state. The agent's objective is to maximize cumulative rewards over time.

6. Policy: A policy is the strategy or rule that the agent follows to determine its actions based on the observed states. It maps states to the probabilities or values of selecting each action.

7. Function: The value function estimates the expected cumulative rewards an agent will receive from a particular state or state-action pair. It guides the agent in assessing the long-term desirability of different actions.

8. Exploration vs. Exploitation: Reinforcement Learning involves a trade-off between exploration and exploitation. Exploration refers to the agent's exploration of new actions to gather information about the environment, while exploitation refers to the agent's utilization of its current knowledge to maximize rewards.

Reinforcement Learning algorithms typically operate through an iterative process of trial and error. The agent interacts with the environment, receives rewards, and updates its policy or value function based on the observed experiences. Popular RL algorithms include Q-Learning, Deep Q-Networks (DQN), Policy Gradient methods, and Proximal Policy Optimization (PPO).

Reinforcement Learning has been successful in various applications. For example, RL has been used to train agents to play complex games like Chess, Go, and video games. RL has also found applications in robotics, where agents learn to control robotic arms or navigate real-world environments. Additionally, RL is used in recommendation systems to learn user preferences and make personalized recommendations.

Reinforcement Learning presents unique challenges, such as balancing exploration and exploitation, dealing with delayed rewards, and handling large state and action spaces. However, it offers a promising approach to training agents that can learn from interactions and make adaptive decisions in complex environments.

In summary, Reinforcement Learning is a subfield of Machine Learning that focuses on training agents to make a sequence of decisions to maximize cumulative rewards in an environment. It involves the interaction between an agent and an environment, with the agent learning through trial and error. RL has applications in game playing, robotics, recommendation systems, and more, and it continues to drive advancements in AI research and practical applications.

CHAPTER 3

The Building Blocks of AI

3.1 Data: The Fuel for AI

Data plays a fundamental role in the development and success of Artificial Intelligence (AI) systems. It serves as the fuel that powers AI algorithms and enables machines to learn, reason, and make accurate predictions. In AI, the quality, quantity, and diversity of data are crucial for training models, evaluating performance, and driving meaningful insights. Let's explore the importance of data in AI and its various aspects:

Training Data:

Training data is a crucial component in AI systems. It consists of labeled or unlabeled examples that are used to train AI models to recognize patterns, make predictions, or perform specific tasks. The quality and representativeness of the training data significantly impact the performance and generalization capabilities of the AI models. Sufficient training data enables models to learn from diverse examples, capture underlying patterns, and make accurate predictions on unseen data.

Labeled Data:

Labeled data refers to training examples that are paired with their corresponding labels or target outputs. For supervised learning tasks, labeled data is essential for training AI models to make accurate predictions. For example, in image classification, labeled data would consist of images with corresponding class labels. Creating high-quality labeled datasets often requires human annotation or expert knowledge to ensure accurate and reliable labels.

Unlabeled Data:

Unlabeled data does not have predefined labels or target outputs. It is commonly used in unsupervised learning, where AI models learn to discover underlying patterns and structures within the data. Unlabeled data is valuable for tasks like clustering, dimensionality reduction, and anomaly detection. Unsupervised learning algorithms can extract meaningful representations from unlabeled data, enabling the discovery of hidden relationships and insights.

Big Data:

The concept of Big Data refers to the vast volume, velocity, and variety of data generated in today's digital age. Big Data provides AI systems with a wealth of information that can be leveraged for training and improving models. Large-scale datasets enable AI algorithms to learn from diverse examples and capture complex relationships within the data. Furthermore, Big Data allows for robust statistical analyses, identification of rare events, and the potential for more accurate predictions.

Data Preprocessing:

Data preprocessing is an essential step in AI, involving cleaning, transforming, and organizing the data before feeding it to AI models. It includes tasks such as removing noise, handling missing values, normalizing features, and balancing class distributions. Proper data preprocessing ensures that AI models are trained on high-quality, consistent, and relevant data, leading to better model performance and generalization.

Data Ethics and Privacy:

As AI relies heavily on data, ethical considerations surrounding data usage and privacy are crucial. AI practitioners and organizations must handle data responsibly, ensuring compliance with privacy regulations and maintaining the security of sensitive information. Respecting data privacy and maintaining transparency in data collection, storage, and usage is essential to foster trust and protect individuals' rights.

Data Collection and Annotation:

Data collection involves gathering relevant data from various sources, such as sensors, databases, APIs, or user interactions. The process may involve designing surveys, deploying data collection systems, or scraping data from the web. Data annotation, on the other hand, involves labeling the collected data with the necessary annotations or metadata for supervised learning tasks. Data annotation may be performed manually or through automated methods, depending on the complexity and requirements of the task.

In summary, data serves as the foundation and fuel for AI systems. It enables the training, evaluation, and performance of AI models, providing the necessary examples and information for learning and decision-making. The quality, quantity, diversity, and ethical handling of data are critical considerations in AI, ensuring accurate predictions, robust insights, and responsible use of AI technologies.

3.2 Algorithms and Models

Algorithms and models are the core components of Artificial Intelligence (AI) systems. They provide the computational framework for processing data, making predictions, and performing tasks. Algorithms define the step-by-step procedures, while models are the mathematical representations that capture patterns and relationships within the data. Let's explore the importance of algorithms and models in AI and some commonly used ones:

Importance of Algorithms and Models in AI:

1. Problem Solving: Algorithms and models enable AI systems to solve complex problems by leveraging data and computational techniques. They provide the structure and logic for understanding, analyzing, and making decisions based on the available information.

2. Pattern Recognition: Algorithms and models allow AI systems to recognize and extract patterns from data. They learn from examples to identify meaningful relationships, which can be used for tasks such as classification, regression, clustering, and anomaly detection.

3. Prediction and Decision Making: AI algorithms and models make predictions or decisions based on the patterns and relationships they have learned from the data. They help in forecasting future outcomes, recommending actions, or determining the optimal course of action in a given context.

4. Adaptability: Algorithms and models can adapt to changing data or environments, allowing AI systems to learn from new information and improve their performance over time. They can update their internal parameters or structures based on feedback and experiences.

5. Efficiency and Scalability: Well-designed algorithms and models optimize the computational efficiency and scalability of AI systems. They ensure that the processing and learning tasks can be performed within reasonable timeframes, even with large datasets or complex problems.

Commonly Used AI Algorithms and Models:

1. Linear Regression: Linear regression is a supervised learning algorithm used for regression tasks. It models the linear relationship between the input features and the target variable to make continuous predictions. It is widely used for tasks such as sales forecasting, price prediction, and trend analysis.

2. Logistic Regression: Logistic regression is a classification algorithm used to predict binary or multiclass outcomes. It models the relationship between the input features and the probability of belonging to different classes. It is commonly used for tasks like spam detection, sentiment analysis, and disease diagnosis.

3. Decision Trees: Decision trees are versatile algorithms that can be used for both classification and regression tasks. They create a hierarchical tree-like structure to make decisions based on feature conditions. Decision trees are interpretable and can handle both numerical and categorical data.

4. Random Forest: Random Forest is an ensemble learning algorithm that combines multiple decision trees to improve accuracy and reduce overfitting. It uses a voting mechanism to make predictions based on the predictions of individual decision trees. Random Forest is used in various domains, including finance, healthcare, and image classification.

5. Support Vector Machines (SVM): SVM is a powerful supervised learning algorithm used for both classification and regression tasks. It maps the input data into a high-dimensional space to find the optimal hyperplane that separates different classes or predicts continuous values. SVM is effective for tasks with complex decision boundaries and limited training data.

6. Neural Networks: Neural networks, especially deep neural networks, have gained significant popularity in recent years. They consist of multiple interconnected layers of artificial neurons that mimic the structure of the human brain. Neural networks excel at learning complex patterns and have been successful in various domains, including image recognition, natural language processing, and speech synthesis.

7. Reinforcement Learning Algorithms: Reinforcement learning algorithms, such as Q-Learning and Deep Q-Networks (DQN), are used in training agents to make decisions and learn optimal policies based on rewards and penalties. These algorithms are commonly used in game playing, robotics, and autonomous systems.

The selection of algorithms and models depends on the specific task, available data, computational resources, and performance requirements. AI practitioners choose the most appropriate algorithm and model combination to achieve accurate predictions, efficient processing, and effective problem-solving in their AI systems.

In summary, algorithms and models are the building blocks of AI systems. They enable problem-solving, pattern recognition, prediction, and decision-making. Different algorithms and models are used for various tasks, such as linear regression, logistic regression, decision trees, random forests, support vector machines, neural networks, and reinforcement learning algorithms. Choosing the right algorithms and models is crucial for achieving accurate, efficient, and scalable AI solutions.

3.3 Training and Learning

Training and learning are essential components of Artificial Intelligence (AI) systems. Training involves the process of teaching AI models to learn patterns and make accurate predictions or decisions. Learning refers to the acquisition of knowledge or skills by AI models through training and experience. Let's explore the key concepts and techniques involved in training and learning AI models:

Training Data:

Training data is a crucial component in training AI models. It consists of labeled or unlabeled examples that are used to teach the models to recognize patterns and make predictions. The quality, representativeness, and diversity of training data significantly impact the performance and generalization capabilities of the AI models.

Training Process:

The training process involves iteratively presenting the training data to the AI model and updating its internal parameters or structures to improve performance. During training, the model receives input data, performs computations, and generates output predictions or decisions. These outputs are compared to the desired outputs (labels) from the training data, and the model's parameters are adjusted to minimize the difference between predicted and desired outputs.

Loss Function:

A loss function, also known as a cost function, quantifies the discrepancy between the predicted outputs and the desired outputs during training. The goal of training is to minimize the loss function, indicating that the model's predictions are close to the true values. Common loss functions include mean squared error (MSE) for regression tasks and cross-entropy loss for classification tasks.

Gradient Descent:

Gradient descent is an optimization algorithm commonly used in training AI models. It calculates the gradient (derivative) of the loss function with respect to the model's parameters and adjusts the parameters in the direction of steepest descent to minimize the loss. It iteratively updates the model's parameters until convergence or a stopping criterion is met.

Backpropagation:

Backpropagation is a key algorithm used to train deep neural networks, a type of AI model with multiple layers. It efficiently calculates the gradients of the loss function with respect to each parameter in the network using the chain rule of calculus. Backpropagation enables the efficient propagation of errors from the output layer to the hidden layers, allowing for effective parameter updates and learning.

Epochs and Batch Size:

During training, the training data is divided into smaller subsets called batches. The model processes each batch, calculates the loss, and updates the parameters. An epoch refers to one complete iteration of the training process, where the model has seen and processed the entire training dataset. Training can involve multiple epochs to improve model performance gradually.

Overfitting and Regularization:

Overfitting occurs when the AI model performs well on the training data but fails to generalize to unseen data. Regularization techniques, such as L1 and L2 regularization, dropout, and early stopping, are used to prevent overfitting. These techniques introduce constraints or penalties during training to reduce model complexity and encourage generalization.

Transfer Learning:

Transfer Learning is a technique where knowledge learned from one task or domain is transferred and applied to another related task or domain. It leverages pre-trained models on large datasets or complex tasks and fine-tunes them on new tasks with limited data. Transfer learning enables faster and more effective learning by leveraging the learned representations from previous tasks.

Continuous Learning:

Continuous learning, also known as lifelong learning or online learning, refers to the ability of AI models to learn from new data and adapt to changing environments. It involves incremental updates to the model's parameters or structures over time without retraining from scratch. Continuous learning allows models to stay up-to-date, handle concept drift, and adapt to new information.

In summary, training and learning are vital processes in AI systems. Training involves teaching AI models to learn patterns and make accurate predictions or decisions using training data. The training process involves optimizing the model's parameters through techniques like gradient descent and backpropagation. Key concepts in training include loss functions, epochs, batch size, regularization, transfer learning, and continuous learning. By training and learning from data, AI models acquire knowledge and skills to perform tasks, make predictions, and adapt to new information.

3.4 Evaluation and Testing

Evaluation and testing are critical stages in the development and deployment of Artificial Intelligence (AI) systems. They help assess the performance, reliability, and generalization capabilities of AI models. Proper evaluation and testing ensure that AI systems meet the desired quality standards and can be trusted to make accurate predictions or decisions. Let's explore the key concepts and techniques involved in evaluating and testing AI models:

Evaluation Metrics:

Evaluation metrics quantify the performance of AI models and provide objective measures to assess their effectiveness. The choice of evaluation metrics depends on the specific task and the desired outcome. Common evaluation metrics include accuracy, precision, recall, F1 score, mean squared error (MSE), and area under the receiver operating characteristic curve (AUC-ROC).

Training and Testing Split:

To evaluate AI models, the available data is typically divided into training and testing datasets. The training data is used to train the models, while the testing data is kept separate and used to assess the model's performance on unseen examples. A common practice is to randomly split the data into training and testing sets, with a larger proportion allocated for training (e.g., 70% training and 30% testing).

Cross-Validation:

Cross-validation is a technique used to assess the performance of AI models when data is limited. It involves splitting the data into multiple subsets or folds, training the model on a combination of folds, and evaluating it on the remaining fold. Cross-validation provides a more robust estimation of model performance by averaging the results across multiple iterations.

Overfitting and Generalization:

Overfitting occurs when an AI model performs well on the training data but fails to generalize to unseen data. To assess generalization, the model's performance on the testing data is evaluated. If the model's performance is significantly worse on the testing data compared to the training data, it indicates overfitting. Techniques like regularization and early stopping can help mitigate overfitting and improve generalization.

Benchmarking:

Benchmarking involves comparing the performance of an AI model against existing baselines or state-of-the-art approaches. It helps establish a reference point for evaluating the model's performance and determining its effectiveness. Benchmarks provide insights into the relative strengths and weaknesses of different models and guide further improvements.

A/B Testing:

A/B testing, also known as split testing, is a technique used to compare the performance of two or more AI models or approaches. It involves randomly assigning users or data samples to different versions of the models and measuring the performance metrics to determine which approach performs better. A/B testing is commonly used in areas like recommendation systems, advertising, and user experience optimization.

Validation Set and Hyperparameter Tuning:

During the training process, AI models often have hyperparameters, which are settings that control the learning process but are not learned from the data. A validation set is used to tune these hyperparameters and find the best combination that maximizes the model's performance. The validation set is separate from the training and testing sets to avoid overfitting to the testing data.

Ethical Considerations:

Evaluation and testing should also consider ethical considerations, such as fairness, bias, and accountability. It is essential to ensure that AI models do not exhibit biased behavior or discriminatory outcomes across different groups. Evaluation should include analyzing performance across different demographic groups and monitoring for any unintended consequences.

In summary, evaluation and testing are crucial stages in AI development. Evaluation metrics, training and testing data splits, cross-validation, benchmarking, and A/B testing help assess the performance and generalization capabilities of AI models. Overfitting, generalization, and hyperparameter tuning are important considerations. Ethical considerations related to fairness, bias, and accountability are also essential in the evaluation and testing process. Proper evaluation and testing ensure the reliability, accuracy, and effectiveness of AI models before deployment.

CHAPTER 4

Machine Learning in Depth

4.1 Supervised Learning

Supervised Learning is a popular and widely used category of Machine Learning where AI models are trained on labeled data, consisting of input examples and corresponding desired outputs. The goal is to learn a mapping or relationship between the input features and the target variable to make accurate predictions or classify new, unseen data. Supervised Learning encompasses various algorithms and techniques that excel in tasks like regression and classification. Let's explore the key concepts and algorithms in Supervised Learning:

Key Concepts in Supervised Learning:

1. Labeled Data: In Supervised Learning, the training data consists of input examples paired with their corresponding labels or target outputs. These labels provide the desired output or ground truth for the given input examples.

2. Input Features: Input features, also known as independent variables or predictors, represent the measurable characteristics or attributes of the data. They serve as the input to the model and influence the predictions or classifications.

3. Target Variable: The target variable, also known as the dependent variable or output, is the variable to be predicted or classified by the model. It can be a continuous value in regression tasks or discrete categories in classification tasks.

4. Training Process: The training process in Supervised Learning involves presenting the labeled training examples to the AI model. The model learns to map the input features to the corresponding target variable by adjusting its internal parameters or structures.

5. Generalization: The objective of Supervised Learning is to create models that can generalize well to unseen data. Generalization refers to the ability of the model to make accurate predictions or classifications on new, unseen examples beyond the training data.

6. Evaluation Metrics: Evaluation metrics are used to measure the performance of Supervised Learning models. Accuracy, mean squared error (MSE), root mean squared error (RMSE), precision, recall, and F1 score are commonly used metrics to assess the model's effectiveness.

Supervised Learning Algorithms:

1. Linear Regression: Linear Regression is a common Supervised Learning algorithm used for regression tasks. It models the linear relationship between the input features and the continuous target variable. The goal is to find the best-fit line that minimizes the difference between the predicted values and the true values.

2. Logistic Regression: Logistic Regression is a popular Supervised Learning algorithm used for binary or multiclass classification

tasks. It models the relationship between the input features and the probability of belonging to different classes. It uses a logistic function to map the input to a probability distribution across classes.

3. Decision Trees: Decision Trees are versatile Supervised Learning algorithms that can handle both regression and classification tasks. They create a tree-like structure of decisions based on feature conditions to make predictions or classifications. Decision Trees are interpretable and can handle both numerical and categorical data.

4. Random Forest: Random Forest is an ensemble learning algorithm that combines multiple decision trees to improve accuracy and reduce overfitting. It utilizes a voting mechanism to make predictions or classifications based on the predictions of individual decision trees. Random Forest is known for its robustness and ability to handle high-dimensional data.

5. Support Vector Machines (SVM): Support Vector Machines are powerful Supervised Learning algorithms used for both regression and classification tasks. They find the optimal hyperplane that separates different classes or predicts continuous values. SVMs are effective for tasks with complex decision boundaries and limited training data.

Supervised Learning has broad applications in various domains, including finance, healthcare, marketing, natural language processing, and image recognition. It is widely used for tasks such as predicting house prices, customer churn prediction, sentiment analysis, spam detection, and object recognition.

In summary, Supervised Learning is a category of Machine Learning where AI models are trained on labeled data to learn the relationship between input features and target variables. Linear regression, logistic regression, decision trees, random forest, and support vector machines are commonly used algorithms. Supervised Learning is effective in regression and classification tasks and finds extensive applications across industries.

4.2 Unsupervised Learning

Unsupervised Learning is a category of Machine Learning where AI models learn from unlabeled data without any predefined target variable. The objective of Unsupervised Learning is to discover underlying patterns, structures, or relationships within the data. Unlike Supervised Learning, there are no explicit labels or desired outputs provided during training. Unsupervised Learning algorithms are particularly useful for tasks like clustering, dimensionality reduction, and anomaly detection. Let's explore the key concepts and algorithms in Unsupervised Learning:

Key Concepts in Unsupervised Learning:

1. Unlabeled Data: Unsupervised Learning algorithms are trained on unlabeled data, where only the input features are available. There are no corresponding labels or target variables provided.

2. Clustering: Clustering is a common task in Unsupervised Learning, where similar data points are grouped together based on their intrinsic similarities. The goal is to identify natural clusters or patterns in the data without prior knowledge of the classes or categories.

3. Dimensionality Reduction: Dimensionality Reduction techniques in Unsupervised Learning aim to reduce the number of input features while preserving the important information. It helps in visualizing high-dimensional data and simplifying the learning process for subsequent tasks.

4. Anomaly Detection: Anomaly Detection involves identifying unusual or abnormal instances in the data that deviate significantly from the expected patterns. Unsupervised Learning algorithms can learn the normal behavior of the data and flag instances that are different or unexpected.

5. Feature Learning: Unsupervised Learning can also be used for feature learning, where the algorithms automatically learn meaningful representations or features from the data. These learned features can then be used for subsequent supervised learning tasks.

Unsupervised Learning Algorithms:

1. K-means Clustering: K-means is a widely used clustering algorithm in Unsupervised Learning. It aims to partition the data into k clusters, where k is a user-defined parameter. K-means assigns data points to clusters based on minimizing the sum of squared distances from the data points to the cluster centroids.

2. Hierarchical Clustering: Hierarchical Clustering builds a hierarchy of clusters by iteratively merging or splitting clusters based on similarity measures. It creates a tree-like structure called a dendrogram, which can be cut at different levels to obtain different clusterings.

3. Principal Component Analysis (PCA): PCA is a popular dimensionality reduction technique in Unsupervised Learning. It transforms high-dimensional data into a lower-dimensional space while preserving the maximum amount of variance. PCA identifies the principal components that capture the most important information in the data.

4. Autoencoders: Autoencoders are neural network architectures used for unsupervised feature learning and dimensionality reduction. They learn to reconstruct the input data from a compressed representation, called the latent space. By training the model to minimize the reconstruction error, the autoencoder learns meaningful representations of the data.

5. Generative Adversarial Networks (GANs): GANs are a class of deep learning models used for unsupervised learning and generative modeling. They consist of two competing networks: a generator network that generates synthetic data, and a discriminator network that tries to distinguish between real and synthetic data. GANs learn to generate realistic data by playing a minimax game between the two networks.

Unsupervised Learning algorithms find applications in various domains, including customer segmentation, image and text clustering, anomaly detection in cybersecurity, and exploratory data analysis.

In summary, Unsupervised Learning is a category of Machine Learning where AI models learn from unlabeled data to discover patterns, structures, or relationships. Clustering, dimensionality reduction, anomaly detection, and feature learning are common tasks in Unsupervised Learning. Algorithms such as k-means, hierarchical clustering, PCA, autoencoders, and GANs are used for unsupervised learning. Unsupervised Learning techniques are valuable for exploratory analysis, data preprocessing, and discovering hidden patterns in the absence of labeled data.

4.3 Semi-Supervised Learning

Semi-Supervised Learning is a hybrid approach that combines elements of both Supervised Learning and Unsupervised Learning. It leverages a combination of labeled and unlabeled data during the training process. While labeled data is costly and time-consuming to acquire, unlabeled data is often abundant and readily available. Semi-Supervised Learning aims to make use of the additional unlabeled data to improve the performance of AI models. It is particularly beneficial when labeled data is scarce or expensive to obtain. Let's explore the key concepts and techniques in Semi-Supervised Learning:

Key Concepts in Semi-Supervised Learning:

1. Labeled Data: Similar to Supervised Learning, Semi-Supervised Learning uses labeled data, where the input examples are paired with their corresponding target variables or labels. Labeled data is typically limited and more expensive to obtain.

2. Unlabeled Data: Unlabeled data in Semi-Supervised Learning refers to the input examples without corresponding labels or target variables. Unlabeled data is abundant and can be easily obtained from various sources.

3. Semi-Supervised Learning Algorithms: Semi-Supervised Learning algorithms aim to learn from both labeled and unlabeled data to improve the model's performance. These algorithms incorporate techniques that utilize the additional information provided by the unlabeled data.

4. Regularization: Regularization techniques, such as self-training, co-training, and multi-view learning, are commonly used in Semi-Supervised Learning. They encourage the model to generalize well by leveraging the relationships between the labeled and unlabeled data.

5. Transfer Learning: Transfer Learning is often employed in Semi-Supervised Learning to transfer knowledge from the labeled data to the unlabeled data. Pre-trained models on labeled data

can be fine-tuned using the unlabeled data, improving the model's performance on the target task.

6. Active Learning: Active Learning is a technique where the AI model actively selects the most informative or uncertain instances from the unlabeled data and queries for their labels. By strategically selecting which instances to label, the model can prioritize obtaining labels for the most useful data points.

Semi-Supervised Learning Techniques:

1. Self-training: Self-training is a technique where an initial model is trained on the labeled data and then used to make predictions on the unlabeled data. The confident predictions of the model on the unlabeled data are then added as pseudo-labels, effectively turning the unlabeled data into labeled data. The model is then retrained using both the original labeled data and the newly pseudo-labeled data.

2. Co-training: Co-training involves training multiple models, each using a different subset of features or views from the input data. The models then exchange information by providing predictions on the unlabeled data that the other model does not have access to. This mutual reinforcement helps the models to learn from the unlabeled data and improve their performance.

3. Generative Models: Generative models, such as Variational Autoencoders (VAEs) and Generative Adversarial Networks (GANs), can be used in Semi-Supervised Learning. These models learn to generate new data that is similar to the training data, effectively learning the underlying distribution of the data. The generated data can then be used to augment the labeled data and improve model performance.

4. Consistency Regularization: Consistency regularization encourages model predictions to be consistent across different perturbations of the same input. By adding noise or making small changes to the input, the model should produce similar predictions. This regularization encourages the model to learn more robust representations and generalizes well to unseen data.

Semi-Supervised Learning has applications in various domains, including natural language processing, computer vision, and speech recognition. It is particularly useful when labeled data is limited or expensive, as it allows AI models to leverage the additional information provided by the large amounts of unlabeled data.

In summary, Semi-Supervised Learning combines labeled and unlabeled data to improve AI model performance. Regularization techniques, transfer learning, active learning, and generative models are commonly used in Semi-Supervised Learning. By utilizing the unlabeled data, Semi-Supervised Learning offers a cost-effective approach to improve model accuracy and generalization in scenarios where labeled data is limited or expensive. e absence of labeled data.

4.4 Supervised vs. Unsupervised Learning

Supervised Learning and Unsupervised Learning are two fundamental categories of Machine Learning approaches. While both are used to extract insights and make predictions from data, they differ in their methodologies, data requirements, and applications. Let's compare Supervised Learning and Unsupervised Learning in key aspects:

Data Requirement:

- Supervised Learning: Supervised Learning requires labeled data, where input examples are paired with their corresponding target variables or labels. The labeled data serves as the basis for training the model to make predictions or classifications.
- Unsupervised Learning: Unsupervised Learning can work with unlabeled data, where input examples do not have corresponding labels or target variables. Unsupervised Learning algorithms focus

on discovering underlying patterns, structures, or relationships within the data without the need for explicit labels.

Objective:

- Supervised Learning: The objective of Supervised Learning is to learn a mapping or relationship between the input features and the target variable based on the provided labeled data. The model is trained to make accurate predictions or classifications on unseen data.
- Unsupervised Learning: Unsupervised Learning aims to discover patterns, structures, or relationships within the data without predefined labels. The goal is to gain insights into the data, identify clusters or anomalies, reduce dimensionality, or learn useful representations.

Training Process:

- Supervised Learning: In Supervised Learning, the training process involves presenting labeled examples to the model, where the input features are paired with their corresponding labels. The model learns from these labeled examples and adjusts its internal parameters or structures to minimize the difference between predicted and desired outputs.
- Unsupervised Learning: In Unsupervised Learning, the training process involves exposing the model to the unlabeled data. The model learns from the inherent structure of the data, identifying patterns or clusters without specific guidance from labeled examples.

Applications:

- Supervised Learning: Supervised Learning is commonly used in tasks that require prediction or classification, such as spam detection, sentiment analysis, fraud detection, image recognition, and language translation. It excels when the desired output or labels are known and available for training.
- Unsupervised Learning: Unsupervised Learning finds applications in tasks like clustering similar data points, dimensionality reduction for visualization or preprocessing, anomaly detection,

recommender systems, and exploratory data analysis. It is useful when the data does not have explicit labels or when discovering hidden patterns is the primary goal.

Performance Evaluation:

- Supervised Learning: Supervised Learning models are evaluated based on their ability to accurately predict or classify unseen data, using evaluation metrics such as accuracy, precision, recall, F1 score, and mean squared error (MSE), depending on the task.
- Unsupervised Learning: Evaluating Unsupervised Learning models is often more challenging since there are no explicit labels for comparison. Evaluation is typically based on criteria like cluster coherence, silhouette score, reconstruction error, or domain-specific measures of goodness.

Hybrid Approaches:

- Semi-Supervised Learning: Semi-Supervised Learning is a hybrid approach that combines elements of both Supervised and Unsupervised Learning. It utilizes both labeled and unlabeled data to enhance model performance. The limited labeled data is supplemented with the abundant unlabeled data, leveraging the benefits of both approaches.

In summary, Supervised Learning and Unsupervised Learning are two distinct approaches in Machine Learning. Supervised Learning requires labeled data for training models to make predictions or classifications, while Unsupervised Learning focuses on discovering patterns and structures from unlabeled data. Each approach has its own strengths and applications, with Supervised Learning excelling in prediction and classification tasks, and Unsupervised Learning being useful for exploring data and extracting insights without explicit labels.

4.5 Feature Engineering

Feature engineering is a crucial process in Machine Learning that involves transforming raw data into meaningful features that can be used by AI models for better prediction or classification. It involves selecting, creating, and transforming features to represent the underlying patterns and relationships in the data. Effective feature engineering can significantly impact the performance and accuracy of AI models. Let's explore the key concepts and techniques in feature engineering:

Feature Selection:

Feature selection involves choosing the most relevant and informative features from the available data. It helps reduce dimensionality, eliminate redundant or irrelevant features, and improve model efficiency. Feature selection techniques include statistical methods, correlation analysis, information gain, and domain knowledge.

Feature Creation:

Feature creation involves generating new features from the existing data. It aims to capture additional information or uncover complex relationships that are not explicitly represented in the original data. Feature creation techniques include polynomial features, interaction terms, transformations (log, square root, etc.), binning, and one-hot encoding for categorical variables.

Feature Transformation:

Feature transformation involves converting or scaling features to improve their distribution, range, or interpretability. It helps to meet the assumptions of the AI models and improve model performance. Techniques include normalization, standardization, logarithmic scaling, and power transformations (Box-Cox transformation).

Handling Missing Data:

Missing data is a common challenge in real-world datasets. Feature engineering techniques are employed to handle missing data, such as imputation methods (mean, median, mode, etc.), creating a separate indicator variable for missingness, or using advanced imputation techniques like multiple imputation or regression-based imputation.

Handling Categorical Variables:

Categorical variables require special treatment in feature engineering, as AI models typically require numerical inputs. Techniques include one-hot encoding, label encoding, target encoding, and frequency encoding. These approaches transform categorical variables into numerical representations that can be effectively used by AI models.

Feature Scaling:

Feature scaling is the process of normalizing the scale or range of features. It ensures that all features contribute equally to the model and prevents certain features from dominating others due to their larger scales. Common scaling techniques include standardization (z-score scaling) and min-max scaling (rescaling features to a specific range).

Feature Extraction:

Feature extraction involves transforming high-dimensional data into a lower-dimensional space by extracting the most important or informative features. Techniques like Principal Component Analysis (PCA), Linear Discriminant Analysis (LDA), and t-SNE (t-Distributed Stochastic Neighbor Embedding) are used to capture the underlying structure of the data and reduce its dimensionality.

Domain Knowledge:

Domain knowledge is essential in feature engineering. It involves incorporating domain-specific insights and understanding to create relevant features. Domain experts can identify relevant variables, interactions, or transformations that can significantly improve model performance and interpretability.

Iterative Process:

Feature engineering is often an iterative process, where initial feature engineering techniques are applied, models are trained and evaluated, and then further refinements are made based on the results. It requires experimentation, data exploration, and feedback from model evaluation to iteratively improve feature engineering choices.

Automated Feature Engineering:

Automated feature engineering tools and techniques, such as feature selection algorithms, genetic programming, and automated machine learning (AutoML) platforms, can assist in automating the process of generating and selecting features, reducing the manual effort involved.

In summary, feature engineering is a critical step in Machine Learning that involves selecting, creating, and transforming features to improve model performance. It encompasses feature selection, creation, transformation, handling missing data, handling categorical variables, scaling, extraction, and leveraging domain knowledge. Effective feature engineering can significantly enhance model accuracy, interpretability, and generalization capabilities.

4.6 Evaluation Metrics

Evaluation metrics are used to assess the performance and effectiveness of Machine Learning models. These metrics provide objective measures of how well the models are performing on a given task. The choice of evaluation metrics depends on the type of task, such as regression or classification, and the specific requirements of the problem at hand. Let's explore some commonly used evaluation metrics in Machine Learning:

Regression Metrics:

1. Mean Squared Error (MSE): MSE measures the average squared difference between the predicted and true values. It provides a measure of the model's overall prediction accuracy, where lower values indicate better performance.

2. Root Mean Squared Error (RMSE): RMSE is the square root of MSE, providing a metric in the original unit of the target variable. It is commonly used when the scale of the target variable is important for interpretation.

3. Mean Absolute Error (MAE): MAE measures the average absolute difference between the predicted and true values. It is less sensitive to outliers compared to MSE and provides a more interpretable metric.

4. R-squared (R^2): R-squared represents the proportion of variance in the target variable that can be explained by the model. It ranges from 0 to 1, where higher values indicate better fit.

Classification Metrics:

1. Accuracy: Accuracy measures the proportion of correct predictions out of the total number of predictions. It is widely used when the class distribution is balanced and provides a simple measure of overall performance.

2. Precision: Precision measures the proportion of true positive predictions out of all positive predictions. It is useful when minimizing false positives is important, such as in medical diagnosis or spam detection.

3. Recall (Sensitivity or True Positive Rate): Recall measures the proportion of true positive predictions out of all actual positive instances. It is useful when minimizing false negatives is critical, such as in disease detection or fraud identification.

4. F1 Score: The F1 score is the harmonic mean of precision and recall, providing a balanced measure between the two. It is commonly used when both precision and recall need to be considered simultaneously.

5. Area Under the Receiver Operating Characteristic Curve (AUC-ROC): AUC-ROC measures the model's ability to discriminate between positive and negative instances across different classification thresholds. It provides an aggregate measure of the model's performance and is useful for imbalanced class distributions.

Clustering Metrics:

1. Silhouette Coefficient: The Silhouette Coefficient measures how well data points fit within their assigned clusters compared to other clusters. It ranges from -1 to 1, where higher values indicate better-defined clusters.

2. Calinski-Harabasz Index: The Calinski-Harabasz Index evaluates the compactness and separation of clusters based on the variance within and between clusters. Higher values indicate better-defined clusters.

3. Davies-Bouldin Index: The Davies-Bouldin Index measures the similarity between clusters based on the average distance between each cluster's centroid. Lower values indicate better-defined clusters.

These are just a few examples of evaluation metrics, and there are many more depending on the specific task and problem domain. It is important to choose evaluation metrics that align with the goals and requirements of the problem being addressed. Additionally, it is advisable to consider the context and potential limitations of each metric when interpreting and comparing model performance.

In summary, evaluation metrics provide objective measures to assess the performance of Machine Learning models. Regression metrics like MSE, RMSE, MAE, and R-squared are used for regression tasks, while classification metrics like accuracy, precision, recall, F1 score, and AUC-ROC are used for classification tasks. Clustering metrics like the Silhouette Coefficient, Calinski-Harabasz Index, and Davies-Bouldin Index evaluate clustering performance. The choice of evaluation metrics depends on the specific task and requirements of the problem.

CHAPTER 5

Deep Learning and Neural Networks

5.1 Introduction to Deep Learning

Deep Learning is a subfield of Machine Learning that focuses on training artificial neural networks with multiple layers to learn hierarchical representations of data. Inspired by the structure and function of the human brain, deep neural networks have demonstrated remarkable success in various domains, including image and speech recognition, natural language processing, and reinforcement learning. In this section, we will explore the fundamental concepts and components of Deep Learning:

Neural Networks:

Neural networks form the foundation of Deep Learning. They are composed of interconnected nodes, called artificial neurons or "units," organized in layers. The layers are typically classified into an input layer, one or more hidden layers, and an output layer. Each neuron receives input signals, performs a computation, and produces an output that is passed to the next layer.

Deep Neural Networks:

Deep neural networks refer to neural networks with multiple hidden layers. These layers enable the network to learn increasingly complex representations of the input data as it propagates through the layers. Deep architectures allow for the extraction of intricate features and the modeling of intricate relationships in the data.

Activation Functions:

Activation functions introduce non-linearities into the neural network, allowing it to learn complex patterns. Popular activation functions include the sigmoid function, hyperbolic tangent (tanh), and rectified linear unit (ReLU). Each activation function has its own characteristics and impacts the network's learning and performance.

Backpropagation:

Backpropagation is a key algorithm used to train deep neural networks. It involves computing the gradients of the network's parameters (weights and biases) with respect to a loss function, using the chain rule of calculus. The gradients are then used to update the parameters, iteratively improving the model's predictions during the training process.

Convolutional Neural Networks (CNNs):

Convolutional Neural Networks are a type of deep neural network specifically designed for processing grid-like data, such as images. CNNs use convolutional layers to apply filters to input data, capturing spatial relationships and extracting meaningful features automatically. They have achieved state-of-the-art performance in tasks like image classification, object detection, and image segmentation.

Recurrent Neural Networks (RNNs):

Recurrent Neural Networks are another type of deep neural network that excels in processing sequential data, such as time series or natural language. RNNs have feedback connections, allowing information to persist and be updated across time steps. This enables the modeling of dependencies and temporal dynamics in the data, making them suitable for tasks like language modeling, machine translation, and speech recognition.

Generative Models:

Deep Learning also includes generative models that can generate new data samples with similar characteristics to the training data. Variational Autoencoders (VAEs) and Generative Adversarial Networks (GANs) are popular examples. These models have applications in image synthesis, text generation, and data augmentation.

Transfer Learning:

Transfer Learning is a technique in Deep Learning that leverages pre-trained models on large datasets or complex tasks and fine-tunes them on new, related tasks with limited data. It allows models to benefit from the learned representations and knowledge acquired during pre-training, enabling faster and more effective learning.

Hardware Acceleration:

Deep Learning models often require significant computational resources to train and make predictions. Graphics Processing Units (GPUs) and specialized hardware, such as Tensor Processing Units (TPUs), are commonly used to accelerate the computations required by deep neural networks. These hardware advancements have greatly contributed to the success and widespread adoption of Deep Learning.

Deep Learning Frameworks:

Various open-source Deep Learning frameworks, such as TensorFlow, PyTorch, and Keras, provide high-level abstractions and tools to build, train, and deploy deep neural networks. These frameworks offer efficient implementations of the algorithms, GPU support, and pre-built models, making it easier for researchers and practitioners to work with Deep Learning.

Deep Learning has revolutionized the field of Artificial Intelligence, enabling significant breakthroughs in tasks like computer vision, natural language processing, and speech recognition. Its ability to learn hierarchical representations from complex data has led to advancements in diverse areas, including autonomous vehicles, healthcare, finance, and robotics.

In summary, Deep Learning is a subfield of Machine Learning that focuses on training deep neural networks with multiple layers to learn hierarchical representations of data. It involves the use of activation functions, backpropagation, and specialized network architectures like CNNs and RNNs. Deep Learning has achieved remarkable success in various domains and is driving significant advancements in AI research and applications.

5.2 Neural Networks: The Basics

Neural networks are the fundamental building blocks of Deep Learning. They are computational models inspired by the structure and function of the human brain, consisting of interconnected artificial neurons or "units." Neural networks learn to perform tasks by adjusting their parameters, such as weights and biases, through a process known as training. Let's explore the basics of neural networks:

Artificial Neurons:

Artificial neurons, also known as nodes or units, are the basic components of a neural network. Each neuron receives input signals, performs a computation, and produces an output. The inputs to a neuron are weighted, and a bias term is added to compute the weighted sum.

This sum is then passed through an activation function, which introduces non-linearity into the network, allowing it to learn complex patterns.

Weights and Biases:

Neural networks have learnable parameters called weights and biases. Weights determine the strength of the connections between neurons, and biases act as an additional input to each neuron. During training, the network adjusts the weights and biases to optimize the model's predictions or classifications.

Layers:

Neurons in a neural network are organized into layers. A neural network typically consists of an input layer, one or more hidden layers, and an output layer. The input layer receives the initial data, and the output layer produces the final output of the network. The hidden layers are responsible for learning representations of the input data through the iterative application of weights and activation functions.

Feedforward Propagation:

Feedforward propagation refers to the process of passing input data through the network from the input layer to the output layer. The inputs are multiplied by the corresponding weights and biases, and the weighted sums are passed through the activation functions in each neuron. This process continues layer by layer until the final output is generated.

Activation Functions:

Activation functions introduce non-linearities into the neural network, allowing it to learn complex patterns and make non-linear transformations of the input data. Popular activation functions include the sigmoid function, hyperbolic tangent (tanh), and rectified linear unit (ReLU). The choice of activation function depends on the problem and the behavior desired in the network.

Training with Backpropagation:

The backpropagation algorithm is commonly used to train neural networks. It involves two main steps: forward propagation and backward propagation. In forward propagation, input data is passed through the network, and the outputs are computed. The computed outputs are then compared to the desired outputs using a loss function. In backward propagation, the gradients of the loss function with respect to the weights and biases are computed using the chain rule of calculus. These gradients are then used to update the weights and biases, iteratively improving the network's performance during training.

Optimization Algorithms:

Optimization algorithms, such as gradient descent, are used to update the weights and biases during training. These algorithms adjust the parameters in the direction that minimizes the loss function, gradually improving the model's predictions. Variations of gradient descent, such as stochastic gradient descent (SGD) and Adam optimizer, are commonly used to accelerate convergence and improve training efficiency.

Deep Neural Networks:

Deep neural networks refer to neural networks with multiple hidden layers. Deep architectures allow for the extraction of hierarchical and abstract representations of the input data. Each hidden layer learns increasingly complex features and relationships, enabling the network to model intricate patterns and make accurate predictions in complex tasks.

Applications of Neural Networks:

Neural networks have shown exceptional performance in various domains, including computer vision, natural language processing, speech recognition, recommendation systems, and many more. They have been successfully applied to tasks like image classification, object detection, machine translation, sentiment analysis, and voice synthesis.

In summary, neural networks are the building blocks of Deep Learning. They consist of interconnected artificial neurons organized into layers. Neural networks learn from data by adjusting weights and biases through training algorithms like backpropagation. Activation functions introduce non-linearity into the network, and optimization algorithms update the parameters during training. Deep neural networks with multiple hidden layers have demonstrated remarkable capabilities in various domains, leading to significant advancements in AI research and applications.

5.3 Convolutional Neural Networks (CNNs)

Convolutional Neural Networks (CNNs) are a specialized type of neural network that excel in processing grid-like data, such as images, by leveraging the spatial relationships and local patterns present in the data. CNNs have revolutionized the field of computer vision and have achieved state-of-the-art performance in tasks like image classification, object detection, and image segmentation. Let's explore the key concepts and components of CNNs:

Convolutional Layers:

Convolutional layers are the fundamental building blocks of CNNs. They consist of filters, also known as kernels or feature maps, which are small matrices that perform a convolution operation on the input data. Convolution involves sliding the filters across the input, element-wise multiplication, and summing the results to produce a feature map. Convolutional layers extract local patterns and features from the input data.

Pooling Layers:

Pooling layers, often used after convolutional layers, downsample the feature maps, reducing their spatial dimensions while retaining the most important information. Max pooling and average pooling are common pooling techniques, where the maximum or average value within each pooling region is retained, respectively. Pooling helps in capturing spatial invariance and reducing the computational complexity of the network.

Activation Functions:

Activation functions introduce non-linearities into the CNN, allowing it to model complex relationships and make non-linear transformations of the data. Common activation functions used in CNNs include the rectified linear unit (ReLU), sigmoid, and hyperbolic tangent (tanh). ReLU is a popular choice due to its ability to mitigate the vanishing gradient problem and accelerate convergence.

Fully Connected Layers:

Fully connected layers, also known as dense layers, are typically present at the end of a CNN. These layers connect every neuron in the previous layer to every neuron in the current layer, allowing for high-level abstraction and complex decision making. Fully connected layers take the features extracted by the preceding convolutional and pooling layers and produce the final outputs of the CNN.

Padding:

Padding is the process of adding additional border pixels to the input data before applying convolution, ensuring that the output feature maps have the same spatial dimensions as the input. Padding helps in preserving spatial information and preventing the reduction of feature map sizes.

Stride:

Stride refers to the step size at which the filters are moved across the input data during convolution. A larger stride results in smaller output feature maps, reducing computational requirements and memory consumption. However, it may lead to the loss of fine-grained spatial information.

Transfer Learning:

Transfer Learning is widely used in CNNs, leveraging pre-trained models on large datasets to boost performance on related tasks with limited data. Pre-trained models, such as those trained on ImageNet, have learned rich and generalized features that can be fine-tuned or used as feature extractors for new tasks. This approach significantly reduces training time and improves performance.

Data Augmentation:

Data augmentation is a technique used in CNNs to increase the diversity and quantity of training data by applying random transformations to the existing data, such as rotations, translations, flips, and color distortions. Data augmentation helps in reducing overfitting and improving the generalization capability of the network.

Applications of CNNs:

CNNs have revolutionized computer vision and have a wide range of applications. They are used for tasks such as image classification, object detection, semantic segmentation, facial recognition, style transfer, and medical image analysis. CNNs have also found applications in natural language processing, such as text classification and sentiment analysis.

In summary, Convolutional Neural Networks (CNNs) are specialized neural networks designed for processing grid-like data, particularly images. They consist of convolutional layers, pooling layers, activation functions, fully connected layers, padding, and stride. CNNs excel in capturing spatial relationships and local patterns, making them highly effective in computer vision tasks. Transfer learning and data augmentation are commonly used techniques in CNNs. CNNs have achieved state-of-the-art performance in various domains and have driven significant advancements in computer vision research and applications.

5.4 Recurrent Neural Networks (RNNs)

Recurrent Neural Networks (RNNs) are a type of neural network specifically designed for processing sequential data, such as time series, text, or speech. RNNs have feedback connections that allow information to persist and be updated across time steps, enabling them to model dependencies and temporal dynamics in the data. RNNs have proven to be highly effective in tasks like language modeling, machine translation, speech recognition, and sentiment analysis. Let's explore the key concepts and components of RNNs:

Recurrent Connections:

The recurrent connections in RNNs allow information to flow from one time step to the next, enabling the network to capture sequential dependencies. The output of a hidden state at time step t serves as an input to the same hidden state at time step t+1, forming a recurrent loop.

Hidden State:

The hidden state in an RNN represents the network's memory or internal representation of the sequential data. The hidden state is updated at each time step based on the input at that time step and the previous hidden state. It carries information from previous time steps, allowing the network to capture context and long-term dependencies.

Vanishing Gradient Problem:

RNNs are susceptible to the vanishing gradient problem, where the gradients become exponentially small as they are backpropagated through time steps. This hinders the network's ability to learn long-term dependencies. Techniques like gated recurrent units (GRUs) and long short-term memory (LSTM) units were developed to mitigate this issue by introducing gating mechanisms that regulate information flow.

LSTM (Long Short-Term Memory) Units:

LSTM units are a type of gated recurrent unit commonly used in RNNs. They have additional memory cells and gating mechanisms that allow them to selectively remember or forget information. LSTMs are effective in capturing long-term dependencies and have become a popular choice for sequential modeling tasks.

GRU (Gated Recurrent Unit):

GRU is another type of gated recurrent unit that simplifies the architecture compared to LSTM while still addressing the vanishing gradient problem. GRUs have reset and update gates that control information flow and allow the network to capture dependencies over long sequences.

Bidirectional RNNs:

Bidirectional RNNs process sequential data not only in the forward direction but also in the reverse direction. This allows the network to capture dependencies in both past and future contexts. Bidirectional RNNs are particularly useful in tasks where future context is important, such as speech recognition and machine translation.

Sequence-to-Sequence Models:

Sequence-to-sequence models, also known as encoder-decoder models, use RNNs to map an input sequence to an output sequence of potentially different lengths. These models are widely used in machine translation, text summarization, and speech recognition, among other tasks.

Teacher Forcing:

Teacher forcing is a technique used during training in sequence-to-sequence models, where the true output sequence is used as input to the decoder, instead of the predicted output from the previous time step. This helps stabilize training and improve convergence.

Applications of RNNs:

RNNs have applications in various domains, including natural language processing, speech recognition, machine translation, sentiment analysis, time series forecasting, and music generation. They are effective in tasks that involve sequential data and dependencies over time.

In summary, Recurrent Neural Networks (RNNs) are specialized neural networks designed for processing sequential data. They have recurrent connections that allow information to flow across time steps, enabling the network to capture dependencies and temporal dynamics. LSTM and GRU units address the vanishing gradient problem and improve the network's ability to learn long-term dependencies. RNNs are widely used in language modeling, machine translation, speech recognition, and other tasks involving sequential data.

5.5 Transfer Learning

Transfer Learning is a technique in Deep Learning that leverages pre-trained models to boost performance on related tasks with limited data. Instead of training a model from scratch, transfer learning allows us to use the knowledge and representations learned by a pre-trained model on a large dataset to aid in solving a different but related task. This approach significantly reduces the training time and computational resources required to achieve good performance. Let's explore the key concepts and benefits of transfer learning:

Pre-trained Models:

Pre-trained models are deep neural networks that have been trained on large-scale datasets, such as ImageNet, which contains millions of labeled images. These models have learned rich and generalized features that capture high-level representations of the data. Popular pre-trained models include VGG, ResNet, Inception, and BERT.

Feature Extraction:

In transfer learning, feature extraction involves using the pre-trained model as a fixed feature extractor. The early layers of the model, which capture low-level features, are retained, and the last few layers, responsible for task-specific representations, are replaced or modified. The input data is passed through the pre-trained model, and the output of the selected layers is used as input to a new classifier or model for the target task.

Fine-tuning:

Fine-tuning extends the feature extraction approach by allowing the weights of the pre-trained model to be further adjusted or fine-tuned on the new task-specific data. In this case, not only the last few layers but also some of the earlier layers are modified during training. Fine-tuning enables the model to learn task-specific patterns while retaining the valuable knowledge learned from the pre-trained model.

Benefits of Transfer Learning:

1. Reduced Training Time: Transfer learning significantly reduces the time required to train a model from scratch. By starting with pre-trained weights, the model already possesses useful initial representations, allowing it to converge faster during training.

2. Improved Performance with Limited Data: Transfer learning is particularly useful when the target task has limited labeled data. The pre-trained model brings prior knowledge from a large dataset, capturing generic features that can be applied to the new task, even with a small number of training samples.

3. Generalization to Unseen Data: Pre-trained models have learned generalized representations from diverse data sources. By leveraging these representations, transfer learning enhances the model's ability to generalize well to unseen data, improving its performance on new, unseen examples.

4. Better Feature Extraction: The early layers of pre-trained models are adept at extracting low-level features, such as edges, textures, and shapes, that are useful across different tasks. Transfer learning enables the use of these valuable feature extractors as a starting point for the new task.

5. Knowledge Transfer: Transfer learning allows the transfer of knowledge learned from one domain to another. Models pre-trained on one domain, such as natural images, can be fine-tuned on a different domain, such as medical images, by learning task-specific features without starting from scratch.

Guidelines for Transfer Learning:

1. Choose a Pre-trained Model: Select a pre-trained model that is suitable for the domain and task at hand. Different models may perform better depending on the nature of the data and the complexity of the task.

2. Decide on Feature Extraction or Fine-tuning: Determine whether to use the pre-trained model as a fixed feature extractor or fine-tune it on the new task-specific data. This decision depends on the size of the target task's dataset and the similarity between the pre-trained and target domains.

3. Adapt Input and Output Layers: Modify the input and output layers of the pre-trained model to match the requirements of the new task. The input size should match the dimensions of the new dataset, and the output layer should reflect the number of classes or desired predictions.

4. Data Augmentation: Augment the available training data with techniques such as rotation, flipping, scaling, or color transformations. Data augmentation increases the diversity and quantity of the training data, which aids in the model's ability to generalize.

Transfer learning has become a widely used technique in Deep Learning, enabling the efficient utilization of pre-trained models and accelerating progress in various domains. By leveraging knowledge gained from large-scale datasets, transfer learning empowers practitioners to build powerful models even with limited data and computational resources.

In summary, transfer learning is a technique that utilizes pre-trained models to improve performance on related tasks with limited data. It leverages the knowledge learned from large-scale datasets and reduces training time. Transfer learning offers benefits such as improved performance, generalization to unseen data, and better feature extraction. By adapting pre-trained models through feature extraction or fine-tuning, transfer learning enables knowledge transfer across domains and facilitates efficient model development.

5.6 Common Deep Learning Architectures

Deep Learning encompasses a variety of neural network architectures designed for different types of data and tasks. These architectures have demonstrated significant success in various domains and have contributed to advancements in fields like computer vision, natural language processing, and speech recognition. Let's explore some of the commonly used deep learning architectures:

Convolutional Neural Networks (CNNs):

Convolutional Neural Networks are widely used for image and video processing tasks. CNNs leverage convolutional layers to apply filters to input data, capturing spatial relationships and extracting meaningful features automatically. They have achieved state-of-the-art performance in tasks such as image classification, object detection, and image segmentation.

Recurrent Neural Networks (RNNs):

Recurrent Neural Networks are designed for sequential data processing, such as time series, text, or speech. RNNs have feedback connections that allow information to persist and be updated across time steps, enabling them to model dependencies and temporal dynamics in the data. RNNs are effective in tasks like language modeling, machine translation, sentiment analysis, and speech recognition.

Long Short-Term Memory (LSTM) Networks:

LSTM Networks are a type of RNN that addresses the vanishing gradient problem and can effectively capture long-term dependencies. LSTMs use memory cells and gating mechanisms to selectively remember or forget information over time, making them suitable for tasks that involve long-range dependencies and context modeling.

Gated Recurrent Units (GRUs):

GRUs are another type of gated recurrent unit that simplifies the architecture compared to LSTMs while still addressing the vanishing gradient problem. GRUs have reset and update gates that control information flow, allowing the network to capture dependencies over long sequences. GRUs are widely used in tasks like language modeling, machine translation, and speech recognition.

Transformer Networks:

Transformer Networks, introduced by the "Attention is All You Need" paper, have revolutionized natural language processing tasks. Transformers use self-attention mechanisms to capture global dependencies and encode contextual information effectively. They have achieved impressive results in machine translation, text summarization, and language understanding tasks.

Generative Adversarial Networks (GANs):

Generative Adversarial Networks consist of a generator network and a discriminator network that play a game against each other. GANs are used to generate realistic synthetic data, such as images or text. They have been successfully applied in tasks like image synthesis, image-to-image translation, and text generation.

Autoencoders:

Autoencoders are neural networks designed for unsupervised learning and dimensionality reduction. They consist of an encoder network that compresses the input data into a low-dimensional representation and a decoder network that reconstructs the original input from the compressed representation. Autoencoders are used in tasks like anomaly detection, denoising, and feature learning.

Siamese Networks:

Siamese Networks are used for tasks involving similarity or distance comparison between inputs. Siamese Networks use two or more identical subnetworks with shared weights to process different inputs. They are commonly used in tasks like facial recognition, signature verification, and similarity-based recommendation systems.

Deep Reinforcement Learning Networks:

Deep Reinforcement Learning Networks combine Deep Learning with reinforcement learning techniques. These networks learn to make sequential decisions by interacting with an environment and receiving rewards or penalties. Deep reinforcement learning has achieved notable success in playing complex games, robotic control, and autonomous navigation.

These are just a few examples of the many deep learning architectures available. Each architecture has its own strengths and is designed for specific types of data and tasks. Researchers and practitioners often customize and combine these architectures to suit their specific needs and achieve optimal performance.

In summary, deep learning architectures such as Convolutional Neural Networks (CNNs), Recurrent Neural Networks (RNNs), Long Short-Term Memory (LSTM) Networks, Transformer Networks, Generative Adversarial Networks (GANs), Autoencoders, Siamese Networks, and Deep Reinforcement Learning Networks have made significant contributions to various domains. Each architecture is designed for specific data types and tasks, pushing the boundaries of Deep Learning research and applications.

CHAPTER 6

The AI Development Process

6.1 Problem Definition and Project Scope

In any AI project, it is crucial to clearly define the problem statement and establish the scope of the project. This helps in setting clear objectives, identifying the target audience, and defining the deliverables. Let's explore the key considerations when defining the problem and scoping an AI project:

Problem Statement:

Start by clearly defining the problem or challenge that the AI project aims to address. The problem statement should be concise and specific, describing the desired outcome or improvement that the AI solution will provide. It is important to understand the problem from various perspectives, including business requirements, user needs, and technical feasibility.

Objectives:

Establish the project's objectives, which outline what you aim to achieve through the AI solution. Objectives should be measurable and aligned with the problem statement. For example, objectives could include improving accuracy by a certain percentage, reducing processing time, or enhancing user experience. Clearly defined objectives serve as benchmarks for evaluating the project's success.

Data Requirements:

Identify the data required to develop and train the AI model. Determine the sources of data, the format and quality of the data, and any data preprocessing or cleaning steps needed. Consider whether existing data is available or if data collection efforts are required. Assess data privacy, security, and compliance considerations.

Target Audience:

Understand the target audience who will benefit from the AI solution. Identify their needs, pain points, and preferences. Tailor the project scope to cater to the specific requirements of the target audience. This could involve designing user interfaces, incorporating specific functionalities, or optimizing the AI model for relevant metrics.

Deliverables:

Define the deliverables of the project, which could include an AI model, a software application, an API, a research paper, or a proof-of-concept prototype. Clarify the expected outputs and outcomes of the project, as well as any project documentation, reports, or presentations that need to be produced. Establish milestones and timelines for each deliverable.

Constraints:

Consider any constraints that might impact the project, such as budget limitations, time constraints, availability of resources, or technical limitations. Evaluate the feasibility of the project within these constraints and assess any potential risks or challenges that may arise.

Ethical and Legal Considerations:

Address ethical and legal considerations relevant to the project, such as data privacy, fairness, bias, transparency, and compliance with regulations. Ensure that the project adheres to ethical guidelines and legal requirements, and establish processes to handle sensitive or confidential data appropriately.

Scalability and Future Expansion:

Anticipate the scalability and potential for future expansion of the AI solution. Consider whether the project can be extended to handle larger datasets, accommodate additional features or functionalities, or adapt to changing requirements. Plan for future iterations and improvements based on feedback and emerging technologies.

Evaluation and Success Metrics:

Define the evaluation metrics and criteria that will be used to assess the success of the project. These metrics should align with the project objectives and problem statement. Establish a methodology for evaluating the performance, impact, and usability of the AI solution, and plan for user feedback and validation.

By defining the problem statement and scoping the project appropriately, you establish a solid foundation for successful AI project implementation. This clarity helps in aligning stakeholders' expectations, guiding the development process, and ensuring that the AI solution effectively addresses the identified problem.

6.2 Data Collection and Preparation

Data collection and preparation are critical steps in AI projects as they lay the foundation for building effective and accurate AI models. Proper data collection ensures that the model receives relevant and representative data, while data preparation involves cleaning, preprocessing, and transforming the data to make it suitable for training the AI model. Let's explore the key considerations in data collection and preparation:

Data Collection Planning:

Define the data collection plan based on the project objectives and requirements. Determine the data sources, such as public datasets, proprietary databases, or data obtained through partnerships. Consider the volume, variety, and velocity of data needed for the project.

Data Relevance and Representativeness:

Ensure that the collected data is relevant to the problem statement and represents the target population or domain of interest. Biases or skewed distributions in the data can affect the model's performance. Strive for diversity and inclusiveness in the data to avoid biased outcomes.

Data Quality:

Assess the quality of the collected data. Identify and address issues such as missing values, outliers, inconsistencies, and inaccuracies. Perform data cleansing operations, such as imputing missing values, removing duplicates, correcting errors, and standardizing formats.

Data Preprocessing:

Preprocess the data to transform it into a suitable format for AI model training. This may involve tasks such as normalization, feature scaling, one-hot encoding, text tokenization, stemming or lemmatization, and handling categorical or ordinal variables. Feature engineering techniques can also be applied to extract meaningful information.

Data Splitting:

Split the data into training, validation, and testing sets. The training set is used to train the AI model, the validation set is used to fine-tune hyperparameters and assess model performance, and the testing set is used to evaluate the final model's generalization ability. Consider the appropriate ratio for splitting the data, ensuring an adequate sample for each set.

Data Augmentation:

If the collected data is limited, consider data augmentation techniques to increase the diversity and quantity of training samples. Augmentation methods may include rotation, flipping, scaling, cropping, adding noise, or introducing variations to the data. Data augmentation can help reduce overfitting and improve model generalization.

Labeling and Annotation:

For supervised learning tasks, annotate or label the data with the ground truth or target values. This process may involve manual labeling, crowdsourcing, or using pre-existing labeled datasets. Ensure labeling consistency and quality control to maintain reliable annotations.

Data Privacy and Security:

Respect data privacy and comply with relevant regulations. Anonymize or de-identify sensitive data to protect individuals' privacy. Establish appropriate security measures to prevent unauthorized access, data breaches, or misuse of the collected data.

Data Versioning and Documentation:

Maintain proper versioning and documentation of the collected data. Document metadata, data sources, preprocessing steps, and any assumptions or biases associated with the data. This documentation aids in transparency, reproducibility, and future reference.

Data Governance and Compliance:

Establish data governance practices to ensure responsible and ethical use of the data. Adhere to legal and regulatory requirements, such as data protection laws, intellectual property rights, and industry-specific regulations. Define data usage policies, access controls, and consent mechanisms.

Proper data collection and preparation are crucial for building accurate and reliable AI models. The quality, relevance, and representativeness of the data significantly impact the model's performance. By following sound data collection practices and applying appropriate preprocessing techniques, you can ensure that the AI model learns from high-quality,

representative data and produces meaningful and trustworthy results.

6.3 Model Selection and Architecture Design

Selecting an appropriate model and designing the architecture are key steps in AI projects. The model choice depends on the problem statement, data characteristics, available resources, and desired performance. The architecture design involves determining the structure, layers, and connections of the model. Let's explore the key considerations in model selection and architecture design:

Problem Understanding:

Gain a thorough understanding of the problem statement, objectives, and requirements. Consider the nature of the data (e.g., image, text, time series) and the task at hand (e.g., classification, regression, sequence generation). Determine whether the problem is better suited for supervised learning, unsupervised learning, or reinforcement learning.

Model Types:

Explore different model types that are relevant to the problem. For example, Convolutional Neural Networks (CNNs) are well-suited for computer vision tasks, Recurrent Neural Networks (RNNs) are effective for sequential data processing, and Transformers excel in natural language processing tasks. Research and evaluate existing models that have achieved success in similar domains.

Complexity vs. Resource Constraints:

Consider the complexity of the model and the available computational resources. More complex models may yield higher accuracy but require more computational power and training time. Balance the desired performance with resource limitations, ensuring that the selected model is feasible within the project's constraints.

Transfer Learning:

Assess whether transfer learning can be utilized. Pre-trained models on large datasets, such as ImageNet or BERT, can be fine-tuned for specific tasks with limited data. Transfer learning can save significant training time and improve performance by leveraging the knowledge and representations learned from pre-training.

Architecture Design:

Design the architecture of the selected model. Determine the number and type of layers, their connectivity, and the size of each layer. Consider factors like depth, width, and the number of parameters in the model. Experiment with different architectures, making adjustments based on the problem requirements and available data.

Hyperparameter Tuning:

Identify the hyperparameters of the model, which are settings that determine the behavior and performance of the model. Examples of hyperparameters include learning rate, batch size, dropout rate, regularization strength, and optimizer type. Conduct hyperparameter tuning to find the optimal values that maximize the model's performance.

Overfitting and Regularization:

Address the issue of overfitting, where the model learns to perform well on the training data but fails to generalize to new data. Implement regularization techniques such as dropout, L1 or L2 regularization, early stopping, or data augmentation. Regularization helps prevent overfitting and improve the model's generalization ability.

Model Evaluation:

Define evaluation metrics to assess the model's performance. Metrics vary depending on the task, but common ones include accuracy, precision, recall, F1 score, mean squared error, or area under the curve. Select metrics that align with the problem statement and objectives. Regularly evaluate the model during training and validation phases.

Model Complexity and Explainability:

Consider the interpretability and explainability of the model. Some models, such as decision trees or linear models, offer more interpretability, enabling easier understanding of the model's decision-making process. Deep learning models are often more complex and less interpretable. Evaluate whether interpretability is crucial for the problem at hand.

Iterative Improvement:

Plan for iterative improvement of the model. Based on evaluation results, refine the model by adjusting the architecture, hyperparameters, or data preprocessing steps. Iteratively fine-tune the model to achieve optimal performance and address any limitations or issues that arise during the development process.

By carefully selecting an appropriate model and designing the architecture, you can build a powerful AI system that effectively addresses the problem statement. Consider the problem requirements, data characteristics, and available resources to make informed decisions. Iteratively refine the model based on evaluation results to continuously improve its performance.

6.4 Training and Fine-Tuning

Once the model architecture is designed, the next step in an AI project is training the model using the available data. Training involves optimizing the model's parameters to minimize a defined loss or error function. Fine-tuning refers to the process of further adjusting the model's parameters to improve its performance. Let's explore the key considerations in training and fine-tuning an AI model:

Data Preparation:

Ensure that the data is appropriately preprocessed and prepared for training. This may involve normalization, scaling, one-hot encoding, or any other preprocessing steps specific to the data type and model requirements. Split the data into training, validation, and testing sets for model evaluation.

Loss Function Selection:

Choose an appropriate loss function that reflects the objective of the problem. Common loss functions include mean squared error (MSE) for regression problems, categorical cross-entropy for multi-class classification, and binary cross-entropy for binary classification. The choice of the loss function depends on the problem statement and the desired behavior of the model.

Optimization Algorithm:

Select an optimization algorithm to update the model's parameters during training. Popular optimization algorithms include Stochastic Gradient Descent (SGD), Adam, RMSprop, and Adagrad. Each algorithm has its own characteristics and hyperparameters that can influence training speed and convergence. Experiment with different optimizers to find the one that works best for the specific problem.

Hyperparameter Tuning:

Tune the hyperparameters of the model and the optimization algorithm to improve performance. Hyperparameters include learning rate, batch size, regularization strength, dropout rate, and the number of training epochs. Perform grid search, random search, or use automated techniques like Bayesian optimization or genetic algorithms to find optimal hyperparameter values.

Training Process:

During training, feed the training data to the model, calculate the loss, and update the model's parameters using backpropagation. Iterate over the training data for multiple epochs, adjusting the model's weights to minimize the loss. Monitor the training process by tracking metrics like training loss and accuracy to evaluate convergence and detect potential issues.

Regularization Techniques:

Apply regularization techniques to prevent overfitting and improve the model's generalization ability. Common regularization techniques include L1 or L2 regularization, dropout, early stopping, and data augmentation. Regularization helps the model avoid memorizing the training data and promotes better performance on unseen data.

Validation and Model Selection:

Periodically evaluate the model's performance on the validation set during training. Use the validation metrics to assess the model's generalization ability and make decisions about further training or stopping criteria. Compare different models or hyperparameter settings based on validation performance to select the best-performing model.

Fine-Tuning:

Fine-tune the model by adjusting the hyperparameters, model architecture, or training process based on the validation results. This iterative process allows for gradual improvement of the model's performance. Experiment with different techniques like learning rate schedules, model ensembling, or transfer learning from related tasks or pre-trained models.

Test Set Evaluation:

Evaluate the final trained model on the independent test set, which represents unseen data. This evaluation provides an unbiased estimate of the model's performance and its ability to generalize to new examples. Compare the test set performance with the validation set performance to ensure consistency and assess any potential overfitting.

Iterative Refinement:

Training and fine-tuning are iterative processes. Analyze the model's performance, identify areas for improvement, and refine the model accordingly. This may involve adjusting the model architecture, modifying hyperparameters, acquiring more data, or exploring advanced techniques.

Throughout the training and fine-tuning process, monitor the model's progress, maintain detailed records, and document the experimentation process. Keep track of the best-performing models, hyperparameters, and training configurations for future reference. Regularly reassess the model's performance and iterate as necessary to achieve the desired outcome.

By effectively training and fine-tuning the AI model, you can optimize its performance, improve generalization, and achieve the desired objectives of the project. The training process is an essential step in developing a robust and accurate AI solution.

6.5 Evaluation and Validation

Evaluation and validation are crucial steps in an AI project to assess the performance and generalization ability of the trained model. These steps help ensure that the model achieves the desired level of accuracy, reliability, and effectiveness. Let's explore the key considerations in evaluation and validation:

Evaluation Metrics:

Define appropriate evaluation metrics that align with the problem statement and objectives. Common metrics include accuracy, precision, recall, F1 score, mean squared error, area under the curve (AUC), or custom domain-specific metrics. Choose metrics that measure the model's performance in a meaningful and interpretable way.

Test Set Evaluation:

Evaluate the trained model on an independent test set that represents unseen data. This provides an unbiased estimate of the model's performance in real-world scenarios. Calculate the chosen evaluation metrics on the test set to assess the model's accuracy and generalization ability. Avoid tuning or modifying the model based on test set results to maintain its integrity.

Cross-Validation:

In cases where data is limited, or the model's performance needs to be more robustly evaluated, consider using cross-validation techniques. Cross-validation involves splitting the data into multiple subsets (folds) and performing multiple rounds of training and evaluation, rotating the folds as test sets. This helps estimate the model's performance with different data partitions.

Validation Set:

During training, use a separate validation set to monitor the model's performance and make decisions about hyperparameter tuning, model selection, or early stopping. Calculate the chosen evaluation metrics on the validation set at regular intervals to assess the model's progress and identify potential issues like overfitting or underfitting.

Overfitting and Underfitting Detection:

Monitor the model's performance on the training and validation sets. If the model exhibits a large gap between training and validation performance, it might be overfitting the training data. Address overfitting by applying regularization techniques, reducing model complexity, or collecting more diverse data. If the model performs poorly on both training and validation sets, it may be underfitting, requiring adjustments to the model architecture or hyperparameters.

Bias and Fairness Assessment:

Evaluate the model for biases and fairness to ensure ethical and unbiased decision-making. Assess whether the model's predictions exhibit disparities across different demographic groups or introduce unintended biases. Analyze the model's performance based on different subgroups to identify potential biases and take corrective measures if necessary.

Confidence and Uncertainty Estimation:

Estimate the model's confidence or uncertainty in its predictions. Some models, such as Bayesian neural networks or ensemble models, can provide uncertainty estimates. Uncertainty estimation helps understand the reliability and robustness of the model's predictions, especially in critical or safety-critical applications.

Error Analysis:

Perform an in-depth analysis of the model's errors to gain insights into its weaknesses and areas for improvement. Identify common types of errors, analyze misclassified examples, and understand the patterns or features that lead to incorrect predictions. This analysis can guide future iterations, data collection, or model enhancements.

User Feedback and Validation:

Solicit feedback from users or domain experts to validate the model's performance. Gather insights into the model's usability, accuracy, and usefulness in real-world scenarios. Feedback can help uncover limitations, identify edge cases, and guide further iterations or improvements.

Documentation and Reporting:

Document the evaluation process, including the evaluation metrics, test set results, cross-validation results, error analysis findings, and user feedback. Create clear and concise reports or presentations that communicate the model's performance, strengths, limitations, and any necessary recommendations or next steps.

By conducting thorough evaluation and validation, you can assess the model's performance, address biases, ensure fairness, and gain confidence in its abilities. Regularly revisit the evaluation process as the model evolves or new data becomes available. Clear documentation and reporting provide transparency and enable stakeholders to make informed decisions based on the evaluation outcomes.

6.6 Deployment and Monitoring

Once an AI model has been trained, evaluated, and validated, the next step is to deploy it into production to make it available for use. Deployment involves integrating the model into an operational system or application, ensuring its robustness, scalability, and ongoing performance. Monitoring the deployed model helps detect issues, track performance, and make necessary improvements. Let's explore the key considerations in deployment and monitoring:

Infrastructure and Environment Setup:

Prepare the necessary infrastructure and environment for deploying the model. This may involve setting up servers, cloud platforms, or edge devices to host and serve the model. Ensure that the deployment environment meets the model's requirements in terms of computational resources, memory, and dependencies.

Model Packaging:

Package the trained model along with any required pre-processing steps, dependencies, and configuration files into a deployable format. This may involve converting the model into a specific file format compatible with the deployment framework or library being used.

Integration with the Operational System:

Integrate the model into the operational system or application where it will be used. This may involve developing APIs, microservices, or modules that expose the model's functionality to other parts of the system. Ensure smooth communication between the model and other system components.

Scalability and Performance Optimization:

Ensure that the deployed model is capable of handling the expected workload and user requests. Optimize the model's performance and resource utilization by leveraging techniques such as model quantization, model compression, or model parallelism. Test the deployment under different load conditions to ensure scalability and responsiveness.

Monitoring Infrastructure:

Implement a monitoring infrastructure to track the performance and behavior of the deployed model. This may involve setting up monitoring tools, logging mechanisms, or visualization dashboards to capture relevant metrics such as response time, throughput, error rates, or resource utilization. Define appropriate alerts and thresholds to detect anomalies or performance degradation.

Performance Monitoring:

Regularly monitor the performance of the deployed model to ensure it meets the desired quality standards. Monitor key metrics, conduct periodic checks, and compare the model's performance against the evaluation results obtained during the development phase. Detect and investigate any deviations or issues that arise.

Error Analysis and Feedback Loop:

Analyze errors and gather feedback from users or system operators to understand any issues or limitations of the deployed model. Identify common failure cases, misclassifications, or edge cases that need attention. Use this feedback to iteratively improve the model, update the training data, or adjust the model's configuration.

Model Maintenance and Updates:

Maintain the deployed model by monitoring changes in the data distribution or user requirements over time. Periodically retrain or update the model to ensure its relevance and accuracy. Implement versioning and tracking mechanisms to manage model updates and maintain consistency.

Security and Privacy Considerations:

Implement security measures to protect the deployed model, data, and user privacy. Apply encryption, access controls, and authentication mechanisms to ensure authorized access and prevent data breaches. Comply with relevant privacy regulations and handle sensitive data appropriately.

Documentation and Knowledge Transfer:

Maintain proper documentation of the deployed model, including its configuration, dependencies, performance metrics, and any updates or modifications. This documentation aids in troubleshooting, knowledge transfer, and future maintenance. Share relevant information with stakeholders and provide support to users or system operators.

Continuous monitoring, maintenance, and improvement of the deployed model are essential to ensure its reliability and effectiveness in production. Regularly assess the model's performance, address any issues that arise, and make necessary updates based on user feedback or changes in the system requirements. By closely monitoring the deployed model, you can proactively identify and resolve issues, optimize performance, and provide a high-quality AI solution to end-users.

CHAPTER 7

Ethical Considerations in AI

7.1 Bias and Fairness

Bias and fairness are critical considerations in AI projects to ensure ethical and equitable outcomes. AI models can inadvertently learn and perpetuate biases present in the data, leading to unfair treatment or discrimination. It is essential to identify and mitigate bias to promote fairness and inclusivity. Let's explore the key concepts and approaches related to bias and fairness in AI:

1. Understanding Bias:

   Bias refers to systematic errors or prejudices in data or model predictions that result in unfair treatment or discrimination against certain individuals or groups. Bias can arise from various sources, including biased data collection, imbalanced data representation, or biased labels. It is important to distinguish between unintentional biases arising from data and those introduced by design or algorithmic choices.

2. Types of Bias:

   There are different types of bias that can manifest in AI systems:

- Sampling Bias: Occurs when the data used for training does not accurately represent the target population, leading to skewed predictions.
- Labeling Bias: Arises when the labeling process introduces bias, either due to subjective judgments, annotation errors, or biases of human labelers.

- Representation Bias: Arises from underrepresentation or misrepresentation of certain groups in the data, leading to unequal treatment.
- Algorithmic Bias: Can occur when the AI model's architecture, features, or learning process introduce bias into the predictions.

3. Fairness:

Fairness in AI refers to the equitable treatment of individuals or groups, ensuring that the model's predictions or decisions are not biased or discriminatory. Fairness aims to prevent disparate impact, where certain groups are systematically disadvantaged, and promote equal opportunities and outcomes for all individuals.

4. Measuring Fairness:

There are several fairness metrics and approaches to measure and evaluate the fairness of AI models:

- Group Fairness: Assess the model's performance across different subgroups defined by sensitive attributes (e.g., gender, race, age) to detect disparities.
- Individual Fairness: Evaluate the similarity of treatment between similar individuals to ensure equal treatment for similar cases.
- Equalized Odds: Evaluate whether the model's predictions have similar false positive and false negative rates across different groups.
- Demographic Parity: Assess whether the model's predictions are independent of sensitive attributes, ensuring equal acceptance rates across groups.

5. Mitigating Bias and Ensuring Fairness:

Mitigating bias and ensuring fairness in AI models is an ongoing process that involves several steps:

- Data Collection: Ensure diverse and representative data collection that accurately reflects the population and avoids underrepresented groups.
- Data Preprocessing: Identify and address biases in the data during preprocessing by carefully handling sensitive attributes and considering fairness constraints.
- Model Development: Regularly assess the model for biases, interpretability, and fairness during development. Employ fairness-aware techniques like regularization, adversarial training, or bias-correction methods.
- Evaluation and Validation: Evaluate the model's performance and fairness using appropriate metrics and fairness tests. Assess the impact of the model on different subgroups and address any disparities.
- User Feedback: Gather user feedback and engage with affected communities to identify potential biases or fairness concerns and take corrective actions.
- Ethical Guidelines: Follow ethical guidelines and standards, such as those provided by regulatory bodies or industry organizations, to ensure fairness and mitigate bias.

6. Transparency and Explainability

   Enhance the transparency and explainability of AI models to understand how they make decisions and detect potential biases. Use interpretable models, provide clear explanations for predictions, or employ techniques like rule-based systems or counterfactual explanations to shed light on the decision-making process.Regular Audits and Updates:

7. Regularly audit and update AI models to detect and mitigate biases that may arise over time. As societal norms evolve, new biases may emerge or existing biases may change. Monitor the performance of the model, evaluate its fairness, and make necessary updates to ensure ongoing fairness and inclusivity.

Addressing bias and promoting fairness in AI is a multidimensional and ongoing effort. It requires a combination of data collection practices, model development techniques, evaluation metrics, user feedback, and adherence to ethical guidelines. By actively considering bias and fairness throughout the AI lifecycle, we can develop AI systems that are more equitable and contribute positively to society.

7.2 Privacy and Security

Privacy and security are essential considerations in AI projects to protect individuals' personal information, maintain data integrity, and ensure ethical and responsible use of AI systems. Safeguarding privacy and implementing robust security measures are crucial to build trust and protect sensitive data. Let's explore the key concepts and approaches related to privacy and security in AI:

1. Data Privacy:

   Respect individuals' privacy rights and comply with relevant privacy regulations. Consider the following practices to protect data privacy:

   - Data Minimization: Collect and retain only the minimum necessary data required for the project, minimizing the potential exposure of personal information.
   - Anonymization and Pseudonymization: Anonymize or pseudonymize data to remove or replace personally identifiable information, reducing the risk of re-identification.
   - Consent and Transparency: Obtain informed consent from individuals when collecting and using their data. Be transparent about data handling practices, including data storage, processing, and sharing.

2. Data Security:

Implement robust security measures to protect data from unauthorized access, breaches, or malicious attacks. Consider the following security practices:

- Encryption: Encrypt sensitive data at rest and in transit to protect it from unauthorized access or interception.
- Access Controls: Implement access controls and authentication mechanisms to ensure that only authorized individuals can access the data and AI systems.
- Secure Infrastructure: Use secure servers, cloud platforms, or edge devices that have appropriate security controls in place.
- Regular Security Audits: Conduct regular security audits and vulnerability assessments to identify and address potential weaknesses in the system.

3. Differential Privacy:Consider employing differential privacy techniques to protect individuals' privacy while extracting insights

   from sensitive data. Differential privacy adds noise or randomness to the data or query results to prevent re-identification and protect individuals' privacy.

4. Secure Data Sharing:

   If data sharing is required, implement secure mechanisms to protect data during transit or collaboration:

- Secure Data Transfer: Use encryption and secure protocols when transferring data between systems or parties to prevent interception or unauthorized access.
- Data Usage Agreements: Establish clear data usage agreements or contracts when sharing data with third parties, specifying limitations on data usage, storage, and retention.

5. Model Privacy:

Consider privacy implications when designing AI models, especially in cases where the model is trained on sensitive data or makes predictions on sensitive attributes. Techniques like federated learning or on-device learning can help maintain data privacy by keeping the data locally and minimizing data exposure.

6. Secure Deployment and APIs:

   Ensure secure deployment of AI models and APIs to protect against potential attacks or vulnerabilities:

   - Secure APIs: Implement authentication, access controls, and rate limiting mechanisms for APIs that expose AI functionality to external systems or users.
   - Model Version Control: Manage model versions and updates securely to prevent unauthorized modifications or tampering.

7. Ethical Considerations:

   Adhere to ethical guidelines and frameworks to ensure responsible AI practices, including privacy and security considerations. This involves considering the potential impact on individuals and society and addressing any ethical concerns related to data collection, usage, and potential biases.

8. User Rights and Transparency.

   Inform users about their rights regarding data usage and provide transparency about how their data is collected, processed, and used. Enable users to access, modify, or delete their data and provide channels for addressing privacy concerns or inquiries.

9. Compliance with Regulations:

   Adhere to relevant data protection and privacy regulations, such as the General Data Protection Regulation (GDPR), California Consumer Privacy Act (CCPA), or sector-specific regulations. Stay updated on evolving regulations and ensure compliance with applicable laws.

10. Employee Awareness and Training:

   Educate and train employees on privacy and security best practices to ensure that they understand their responsibilities and follow proper data handling procedures. Create a culture of privacy and security within the organization.

By prioritizing privacy and security throughout the AI project lifecycle, you can protect individuals' privacy rights, maintain data integrity, and build trust in AI systems. Incorporate privacy and security measures at each stage, from data collection and model development to deployment and ongoing maintenance. Safeguarding privacy and ensuring robust security practices are fundamental to responsible and trustworthy AI implementation.

7.3 Transparency and Explainability

Transparency and explainability are important considerations in AI projects to promote trust, accountability, and ethical decision-making. Transparency refers to making the AI system's operations and processes understandable and accessible, while explainability focuses on providing understandable explanations for the system's decisions. Let's explore the key concepts and approaches related to transparency and explainability in AI:

1. Model Transparency:

   Strive to make the AI model's operations and inner workings transparent to the extent possible. Enhance model transparency through the following practices:

- Documentation: Document the model architecture, hyperparameters, and training process, providing detailed information on how the model was developed.
- Model Visualization: Visualize the model's structure, layers, and connections to aid in understanding its behavior.
- Interpretability Techniques: Employ techniques such as feature importance analysis, saliency maps, or attention mechanisms to reveal the model's decision-making process.

2. Explainable AI (XAI):

   Develop AI systems that can provide understandable explanations for their decisions or predictions. This can be particularly important in high-stakes or regulated domains. Consider the following approaches for explainability:

   - Rule-based Systems: Use rule-based models or decision trees that provide explicit and interpretable rules for decision-making.
   - Feature Importance: Assess and communicate the importance of input features in the model's predictions to understand its decision factors.
   - Local Explanations: Provide explanations at the instance level to explain why a specific decision or prediction was made.
   - Counterfactual Explanations: Generate alternative scenarios that would have led to different outcomes, helping users understand the factors driving the model's decisions.

3. Ethical Considerations:

   Ensure that transparency and explainability efforts align with ethical guidelines and considerations. Strive for transparency without compromising privacy or exposing sensitive information. Avoid explanations that may perpetuate biases or discriminate against certain groups.

4. User-Friendly Interfaces:

   Design user-friendly interfaces that facilitate user understanding of the AI system's operations and explanations. Provide visualizations, interactive components, or natural language explanations to make the information more accessible and interpretable.

5. Contextual Explanations:

Consider providing explanations in a context-specific manner, tailoring them to the needs and backgrounds of different user groups. Explanations can be adapted based on user expertise, domain knowledge, or individual preferences to improve understanding and trust.

6. Evaluation of Explainability:

   Develop evaluation methods to assess the quality and effectiveness of the explanations provided by the AI system. Conduct user studies, surveys, or interviews to gauge user understanding, trust, and satisfaction with the explanations. Continuously refine and improve the explainability techniques based on user feedback.

7. Regulatory Compliance:

   Be aware of regulatory requirements related to transparency and explainability, especially in regulated domains or regions. Understand and comply with relevant regulations, such as the General Data Protection Regulation (GDPR) or specific industry guidelines, to ensure transparency and accountability.

8. Ongoing Research and Development:

   Stay up to date with research advancements in explainable AI and transparency techniques. Explore emerging methods and approaches that enhance transparency and provide more meaningful explanations. Foster collaboration between researchers, practitioners, and policymakers to address the challenges and opportunities in this field.

9. Communication and Education:

   Communicate with stakeholders, users, and the general public about the AI system's operations, limitations, and potential biases. Educate users and decision-makers about the benefits and trade-offs of transparency and explainability, promoting awareness and understanding of AI systems' capabilities and limitations.

10. Iterative Improvement:

Continuously improve the transparency and explainability of the AI system through iterative development and user feedback. Regularly assess the effectiveness of the transparency and explainability techniques and incorporate improvements based on user needs, domain requirements, and ethical considerations.

By prioritizing transparency and explainability, AI systems can foster trust, facilitate better decision-making, and address concerns related to bias, discrimination, or lack of accountability. Strive to make the AI system's operations and decision-making process transparent, and provide understandable explanations to users. This promotes responsible and ethical AI deployment while empowering users to trust, validate, and challenge the AI system's decisions.

7.4 Accountability and Governance

Accountability and governance are critical aspects of AI projects to ensure responsible and ethical use of AI systems. Accountability refers to the obligation to take responsibility for the actions, decisions, and consequences of AI systems, while governance involves establishing policies, guidelines, and mechanisms to regulate and oversee AI development and deployment. Let's explore the key concepts and approaches related to accountability and governance in AI:

Ethical Guidelines and Frameworks:

Adopt and adhere to established ethical guidelines and frameworks that promote responsible AI development and deployment. Examples include the IEEE Ethically Aligned Design, the AI Principles of organizations like OpenAI or the Partnership on AI, or regulatory guidelines like the European Commission's Ethics Guidelines for Trustworthy AI.

Responsible AI Principles:

Define and adhere to a set of responsible AI principles that align with your organization's values and objectives. These principles may include transparency, fairness, privacy protection, safety, explainability, and human-centered design. Use these principles as guiding principles throughout the AI project lifecycle.

Clear Roles and Responsibilities:

Establish clear roles and responsibilities for individuals and teams involved in AI projects. Clearly define who is accountable for the development, deployment, monitoring, and maintenance of AI systems. Assign responsibility for ensuring ethical considerations, including bias mitigation, privacy protection, and adherence to regulations.

Regulatory Compliance:

Understand and comply with relevant laws, regulations, and industry standards governing AI development and deployment. Ensure compliance with data protection and privacy regulations, intellectual property rights, anti-discrimination laws, and any sector-specific regulations that may apply.

Risk Assessment and Mitigation:

Conduct a comprehensive risk assessment to identify potential risks and ethical considerations associated with the AI system. Assess risks related to bias, privacy, security, fairness, safety, and unintended consequences. Develop risk mitigation strategies and incorporate them into the project plan.

Human-in-the-Loop Approach:

Consider implementing a human-in-the-loop approach, where human oversight and intervention are integrated into AI systems. This approach enables human experts to monitor, validate, and correct the system's outputs, ensuring accountability and reducing the impact of errors or biases.

Continuous Monitoring and Auditing:

Implement mechanisms for continuous monitoring and auditing of AI systems. Regularly assess the system's performance, fairness, bias, privacy compliance, and adherence to ethical guidelines. Conduct regular audits to evaluate the system's impact, identify potential issues, and take corrective actions.

User Feedback and Redress:

Establish channels for users and stakeholders to provide feedback, raise concerns, or seek redress related to the AI system's decisions or impact. Actively listen to user feedback, address concerns, and take appropriate actions to rectify any issues that may arise.

Education and Awareness:

Promote education and awareness about AI ethics, responsible AI practices, and potential societal impacts among stakeholders, employees, and the general public. Foster a culture of responsible AI by providing training, resources, and guidelines to ensure that all individuals involved in AI projects understand the ethical considerations and their responsibilities.

External Oversight and Independent Review:

Consider engaging external experts or third-party organizations for independent oversight, audits, or reviews of AI systems. External perspectives can provide valuable insights, impartial evaluations, and recommendations for improvement.

Ethical Review Boards:

Establish internal ethical review boards or committees to review and evaluate the ethical implications of AI projects. These boards can provide guidance, ensure adherence to ethical principles, and make recommendations on complex ethical dilemmas.

Iterative Improvement and Learning:

Continuously learn from experiences and iterate on AI systems based on feedback, insights, and new knowledge. Embrace a culture of continuous improvement, fostering innovation while ensuring responsible and ethical AI practices.

By prioritizing accountability and governance in AI projects, you can foster responsible AI development, mitigate risks, and ensure that AI systems align with ethical principles and legal requirements. Establish clear roles and responsibilities, adhere to ethical guidelines, and engage in continuous monitoring, auditing, and improvement. Through transparent and responsible practices, AI systems can contribute positively to society while being accountable for their impact and decisions.

CHAPTER 8

The Future of AI

8.1 AI in Industry and Business

Artificial Intelligence (AI) has become a transformative technology across various industries and has the potential to revolutionize business operations, decision-making processes, and customer experiences. Let's explore the applications and benefits of AI in different industry sectors:

Healthcare:

AI is transforming healthcare by improving diagnostics, patient care, and medical research. It enables faster and more accurate diagnosis through medical imaging analysis, assists in predicting disease outcomes, supports drug discovery, and aids in personalized medicine. AI-powered chatbots and virtual assistants enhance patient engagement and provide healthcare information and support.

Finance and Banking:

In the financial sector, AI is used for fraud detection, risk assessment, algorithmic trading, customer service, and personalized banking experiences. AI models analyze vast amounts of financial data to detect anomalies, predict market trends, automate credit scoring, and optimize investment portfolios. Chatbots and virtual assistants provide real-time customer support and assistance.

Retail and E-commerce:

AI is revolutionizing the retail and e-commerce industry by enabling personalized shopping experiences, demand forecasting, inventory management, and recommendation systems. AI-powered chatbots handle customer queries and provide product recommendations. Computer vision technologies enhance visual search capabilities, allowing customers to find products using images.

Manufacturing and Supply Chain:

AI is enhancing efficiency and productivity in manufacturing and supply chain operations. It enables predictive maintenance, quality control, and optimized production processes through real-time data analysis. AI-powered algorithms help optimize inventory management, logistics, and route planning to reduce costs and streamline operations.

Transportation and Logistics:

AI is transforming the transportation and logistics industry through autonomous vehicles, route optimization, and predictive maintenance. AI-powered algorithms analyze real-time data to optimize transportation routes, improve fuel efficiency, and enhance traffic management. Autonomous vehicles and drones are being developed for delivery and logistics purposes.

Energy and Utilities:

AI is helping the energy and utilities sector improve efficiency, reduce costs, and optimize energy consumption. AI-powered systems analyze energy data to optimize power generation and distribution, predict maintenance needs, and improve energy grid management. Smart grids, energy monitoring, and demand response systems are enabled by AI technologies.

Agriculture:

AI is driving innovation in agriculture by enabling precision farming, crop monitoring, and yield optimization. AI-powered drones, sensors, and satellite imagery analyze agricultural data to optimize irrigation, fertilization, and pest control. AI algorithms provide insights for optimal planting, harvesting, and resource management, leading to increased crop yield and sustainability.

Human Resources and Recruitment:

AI is streamlining human resources processes, including recruitment, candidate screening, and employee engagement. AI-powered tools automate resume screening, conduct sentiment analysis during interviews, and assist in talent management. Chatbots provide HR support and answer employee queries.

Marketing and Advertising:

AI enhances marketing and advertising strategies through personalized targeting, sentiment analysis, and content optimization. AI-powered algorithms analyze customer data to deliver personalized recommendations and targeted advertisements. Natural language processing and sentiment analysis help gauge customer sentiment and optimize marketing campaigns.

Customer Service:

AI-powered chatbots and virtual assistants improve customer service by providing real-time support, answering queries, and resolving issues. Natural language processing allows chatbots to understand and respond to customer inquiries, enhancing the overall customer experience and reducing the need for human intervention.

The applications of AI are vast and continue to expand across industries, enabling automation, optimization, and innovation. Organizations that leverage AI can gain a competitive edge, improve operational efficiency, enhance customer experiences, and drive growth. However, it is important to address ethical considerations, data privacy, and accountability when implementing AI solutions in business settings.

8.2 AI in Healthcare

Artificial Intelligence (AI) is revolutionizing the healthcare industry by transforming medical research, diagnosis, treatment, and patient care. AI-powered systems and algorithms analyze vast amounts of data, make predictions, and provide insights to support healthcare professionals in delivering more accurate and personalized care. Here are some key applications of AI in healthcare:

Medical Imaging Analysis:

AI algorithms analyze medical images such as X-rays, CT scans, MRIs, and mammograms to assist in the detection and diagnosis of diseases. Deep learning models can detect patterns, anomalies, and early signs of diseases, aiding radiologists in making more accurate and timely diagnoses.

Disease Diagnosis and Prognosis:

AI helps in diagnosing and predicting diseases by analyzing patient data, medical records, and genetic information. Machine learning models can identify patterns, risk factors, and genetic markers associated with specific diseases. This assists healthcare professionals in making more accurate diagnoses and predicting disease outcomes.

Precision Medicine:

AI facilitates personalized medicine by analyzing patient data, genetic information, and medical literature to identify targeted treatments and therapies. AI algorithms can analyze genetic profiles to determine the most effective drugs or treatment plans based on individual characteristics, improving treatment outcomes and minimizing adverse effects.

Drug Discovery and Development:

AI accelerates the drug discovery and development process by analyzing vast amounts of biomedical data, scientific literature, and molecular structures. Machine learning models assist in identifying potential drug candidates, predicting drug efficacy, and simulating drug interactions, reducing the time and cost required for drug discovery.

Virtual Assistants and Chatbots:

AI-powered virtual assistants and chatbots provide 24/7 support and guidance to patients. These systems can answer general health-related questions, provide medication reminders, schedule appointments, and triage patient inquiries, reducing the burden on healthcare professionals and improving patient access to healthcare information.

Electronic Health Records (EHR) Management:

AI algorithms can analyze electronic health records to extract relevant information, detect patterns, and identify potential risks or treatment gaps. This improves the accuracy and efficiency of EHR management, assists in clinical decision-making, and supports population health management.

Robotics and Surgical Assistance:

AI-enabled robotic systems assist surgeons in performing complex surgical procedures with precision and accuracy. These robotic systems can enhance surgical outcomes, minimize invasiveness, and reduce recovery times. AI algorithms also aid in surgical planning, image-guided procedures, and real-time monitoring during surgery.

Health Monitoring and Wearable Devices:

AI algorithms analyze data from wearable devices, such as fitness trackers and smartwatches, to monitor and assess an individual's health status. This enables proactive health monitoring, early detection of abnormalities, and personalized health recommendations. AI can also assist in analyzing data from implantable devices for cardiac or neurological conditions.

Health Risk Assessment and Predictive Analytics:

AI models can assess individual health risks by analyzing various factors such as lifestyle, genetics, medical history, and environmental data. Predictive analytics techniques help identify individuals at high risk of developing certain diseases, enabling proactive interventions, and preventive care.

Public Health Surveillance:

AI contributes to public health surveillance by analyzing large-scale data, such as social media posts, news articles, and electronic health records, to detect disease outbreaks, monitor the spread of infectious diseases, and provide early warning systems. This aids in timely response and effective public health interventions.

AI in healthcare holds immense potential for improving patient outcomes, enhancing efficiency, and advancing medical research. However, it is important to address ethical considerations, data privacy, regulatory compliance, and ensure proper validation and integration of AI systems into clinical workflows. Collaboration between AI experts, healthcare professionals, and regulatory bodies is crucial to ensure responsible and effective use of AI in healthcare.

8.3 AI in Transportation

Artificial Intelligence (AI) is transforming the transportation industry by enabling automation, optimizing operations, improving safety, and enhancing the overall efficiency of transportation systems. From autonomous vehicles to traffic management, AI technologies are reshaping how people and goods move. Here are some key applications of AI in transportation:

Autonomous Vehicles:

AI plays a vital role in the development of autonomous vehicles. AI algorithms, including computer vision, machine learning, and sensor fusion, enable vehicles to perceive their surroundings, make decisions, and navigate safely without human intervention. Autonomous vehicles have the potential to enhance road safety, reduce congestion, and provide accessible transportation options.

Traffic Management:

AI-powered systems assist in optimizing traffic flow and managing congestion. AI algorithms analyze real-time traffic data, including vehicle speeds, traffic volumes, and road conditions, to predict and mitigate traffic congestion. Intelligent transportation systems use AI to optimize traffic signal timing, adaptive traffic control, and dynamic route guidance to improve traffic efficiency.

Intelligent Transportation Systems (ITS):

AI facilitates the development of intelligent transportation systems that enhance road safety, efficiency, and sustainability. ITS integrates AI technologies, including vehicle-to-vehicle (V2V) and vehicle-to-infrastructure (V2I) communication, advanced driver assistance systems (ADAS), and predictive analytics to enable cooperative and connected transportation systems.

Fleet Management and Logistics:

AI-powered systems optimize fleet management and logistics operations. AI algorithms analyze data on routes, traffic conditions, delivery schedules, and vehicle performance to optimize delivery routes, reduce fuel consumption, improve operational efficiency, and minimize transportation costs. Predictive analytics helps in demand forecasting and inventory management.

Smart Parking:

AI-based systems assist drivers in finding available parking spaces efficiently. AI algorithms analyze real-time data from sensors, cameras, and parking occupancy information to guide drivers to the nearest vacant parking spots, reducing the time spent searching for parking. This improves traffic flow and reduces congestion in urban areas.

Predictive Maintenance:

AI algorithms analyze sensor data from vehicles, trains, or airplanes to predict maintenance needs and identify potential equipment failures. Predictive maintenance helps optimize maintenance schedules, reduce downtime, and ensure the reliability and safety of transportation assets. This can save costs and improve operational efficiency.

Customer Experience:

AI enhances the customer experience in transportation. Natural Language Processing (NLP) and chatbot technologies assist passengers in accessing travel information, providing real-time updates, answering queries, and offering personalized recommendations. AI-powered voice assistants in vehicles enable hands-free control and provide a more intuitive and convenient travel experience.

Transportation Security:

AI technologies, such as video analytics and facial recognition, improve security in transportation systems. AI algorithms analyze video feeds from surveillance cameras to detect potential security threats, monitor passenger behavior, and identify unauthorized access. These technologies enhance public safety and aid in emergency response.

Traffic Accident Prevention:

AI-based systems analyze historical accident data, road conditions, weather forecasts, and sensor data to identify accident-prone areas and predict potential hazards. This enables proactive measures such as improved signage, road design modifications, or traffic control adjustments to prevent accidents and improve road safety.

Ride-Sharing and Mobility Services:

AI powers ride-sharing and mobility services by matching passengers with drivers, optimizing routes, and calculating fares. AI algorithms consider factors such as passenger preferences, traffic conditions, and demand patterns to provide efficient and convenient transportation options. This helps reduce congestion, improve resource utilization, and enhance the overall mobility experience.

AI's impact on the transportation industry is vast, enabling advancements in safety, efficiency, and sustainability. However, it is crucial to address ethical considerations, privacy concerns, and regulatory frameworks to ensure responsible and secure deployment of AI technologies in transportation systems. Collaboration among transportation stakeholders, AI developers, and policymakers is essential for the successful integration and implementation of AI in the transportation sector.

8.4 AI in Education

Artificial Intelligence (AI) is transforming the field of education by offering innovative solutions that enhance teaching and learning experiences, improve educational outcomes, and enable personalized education. AI-powered tools and applications are being integrated into educational institutions to support educators, engage students, and provide data-driven insights. Here are some key applications of AI in education:

Personalized Learning:

AI enables personalized learning experiences tailored to the individual needs and preferences of students. Adaptive learning platforms use AI algorithms to analyze student performance, track learning progress, and provide customized content and recommendations. This helps students learn at their own pace, focusing on areas where they need the most support.

Intelligent Tutoring Systems:

AI-powered tutoring systems provide individualized guidance and support to students. These systems assess students' knowledge, provide real-time feedback, and adapt instructional content based on their learning needs. Intelligent tutoring systems can simulate one-on-one tutoring, providing personalized attention and assistance.

Virtual Assistants and Chatbots:

AI-powered virtual assistants and chatbots assist students and educators by answering questions, providing educational resources, and offering guidance. These tools can handle routine inquiries, freeing up educators' time for more personalized interactions with students. They enhance accessibility and support a more engaging learning environment.

Automated Grading and Feedback:

AI algorithms can automate grading and provide feedback on assignments and assessments. Machine learning models can analyze student responses, essays, and code submissions to provide immediate feedback and identify areas for improvement. This speeds up the grading process, reduces the burden on educators, and enables timely feedback to students.

Smart Content and Resource Recommendations:

AI-powered systems analyze educational content, learning resources, and student preferences to provide tailored recommendations. These systems suggest relevant materials, learning activities, and resources to support students' learning journeys. This ensures students have access to high-quality, personalized learning materials.

Learning Analytics:

AI enables the analysis of large datasets to extract insights about student learning patterns, performance, and engagement. Learning analytics can identify at-risk students, track progress, and provide early intervention strategies. Educators can leverage these insights to make data-informed decisions, adapt instructional strategies, and support student success.

Natural Language Processing (NLP) in Language Learning:

NLP technologies assist in language learning by analyzing and processing natural language. AI-powered language learning platforms can provide pronunciation feedback, language translation, grammar correction, and conversational practice. These tools enhance language learning experiences and support learners at various proficiency levels.

Educational Content Creation:

AI can assist in generating educational content and resources. Natural language generation algorithms can automatically create summaries, explanations, or practice questions from existing educational materials or datasets. This speeds up content creation processes and expands the availability of educational resources.

Early Intervention and Special Needs Support:

AI systems can identify early warning signs of learning difficulties or special needs in students. Machine learning models analyze student data, behaviors, and performance to detect potential challenges and provide early intervention strategies. AI tools can support personalized interventions and accommodations for students with special needs.

Educational Research and Insights:

AI algorithms assist researchers in analyzing educational data, conducting data-driven studies, and generating insights. AI enables large-scale data analysis, identifying patterns, correlations, and trends in educational research. These insights can inform evidence-based practices and policy decisions in education.

The integration of AI in education holds significant potential to improve educational experiences, enhance personalized learning, and support educators in their instructional practices. However, it is crucial to address ethical considerations, data privacy, and the need for human guidance and interaction. Collaboration between AI experts, educators, policymakers, and stakeholders is essential to ensure the responsible and effective use of AI in education.

8.5 AI and Job Automation

Artificial Intelligence (AI) and automation technologies have the potential to reshape the job market by automating repetitive tasks, improving efficiency, and augmenting human capabilities. While AI can create new job opportunities, it can also lead to job displacement and shifts in the labor market. Here are key considerations regarding AI and job automation:

Job Automation Potential:

AI technologies, such as machine learning, robotics, and natural language processing, can automate tasks traditionally performed by humans. Jobs that involve repetitive, rule-based tasks with well-defined patterns are more susceptible to automation. Routine tasks in manufacturing, customer service, data entry, and transportation are among those most likely to be affected.

Task Augmentation:

AI technologies can also augment human capabilities, enabling workers to perform their jobs more effectively and efficiently. AI-powered tools and software can assist in data analysis, decision-making, customer support, and process automation, empowering workers to focus on higher-value tasks that require human creativity, problem-solving, and emotional intelligence.

Skill Shifts and Job Evolution:

As automation progresses, the job market undergoes shifts that require workers to adapt and acquire new skills. While certain job roles may decline, new roles emerge that involve managing AI systems, analyzing and interpreting AI-generated insights, and developing AI technologies. Upskilling and reskilling programs are essential to ensure workers can transition to new roles.

Human-AI Collaboration:

Collaboration between humans and AI systems becomes crucial. AI can handle data processing, pattern recognition, and repetitive tasks, while humans contribute critical thinking, creativity, empathy, and complex problem-solving abilities. Jobs that involve human interaction, creativity, and adaptability, such as healthcare, education, and social services, are less likely to be fully automated.

New Job Opportunities:

AI also creates new job opportunities. The development, implementation, and maintenance of AI technologies require skilled professionals in fields such as AI research, data science, machine learning, and AI ethics. Additionally, as industries evolve with AI adoption, new roles emerge to manage and leverage AI systems effectively.

Ethical Considerations:

The ethical implications of job automation need to be carefully considered. Issues like job displacement, worker well-being, and income inequality should be addressed. Governments, businesses, and educational institutions play a crucial role in ensuring a smooth transition, supporting affected workers, and providing opportunities for skill development and reemployment.

Lifelong Learning:

In an AI-driven job market, continuous learning and upskilling are essential for individuals to remain relevant. Developing skills that complement AI technologies, such as critical thinking, problem-solving, creativity, and emotional intelligence, can enhance employability and adaptability in the evolving job landscape.

Social and Economic Impacts:

AI-driven automation may lead to shifts in income distribution and job polarization. Policymakers need to consider measures such as social safety nets, income support, and retraining programs to address potential challenges arising from job displacement and ensure equitable access to new job opportunities.

Collaboration and Dialogue:

Stakeholders from academia, industry, government, and labor organizations should collaborate to understand the impacts of AI on the job market and develop policies that foster responsible AI adoption. Open dialogue and engagement with affected communities are essential to shape the future of work in an AI-driven era.

Job Redesign and Value Creation:

As automation takes over repetitive tasks, job redesign becomes crucial. Organizations should focus on creating roles that emphasize creativity, problem-solving, relationship-building, and strategic decision-making. This allows humans to leverage AI technologies to drive innovation, enhance customer experiences, and create new value.

AI and automation will undoubtedly impact the job market, but the extent and nature of these effects will vary across industries and job roles. Adapting to these changes requires a proactive approach, investment in human capital, and collaboration to ensure a fair and inclusive transition to the AI-driven future of work.

8.6 Ethical Challenges and Opportunities

The widespread adoption of Artificial Intelligence (AI) presents both ethical challenges and opportunities. It is important to address these challenges to ensure responsible and beneficial use of AI technologies. Here are some key ethical considerations:

Bias and Fairness:

AI systems can inherit biases present in the data they are trained on, leading to unfair or discriminatory outcomes. It is crucial to address bias in data, algorithms, and decision-making processes to ensure fairness and prevent discrimination based on factors such as race, gender, or socioeconomic status. Regular audits and transparency in algorithmic decision-making can help mitigate bias.

Privacy and Data Protection:

AI relies on vast amounts of data, often including personal and sensitive information. Safeguarding privacy and protecting data is essential. Organizations must adhere to privacy regulations, obtain informed consent, and implement robust security measures to protect individuals' data from unauthorized access, breaches, or misuse. Privacy-preserving AI techniques, such as differential privacy, can help balance privacy concerns with data utility.

Transparency and Explainability:

AI algorithms and systems should be transparent and explainable, allowing users to understand the reasoning behind decisions. Explainable AI (XAI) techniques enable users to comprehend the factors influencing AI outputs, fostering trust, accountability, and reducing the "black box" nature of AI. Transparent disclosure of AI use, data handling practices, and potential limitations is vital.

Accountability and Governance:

Clear roles and responsibilities need to be established to ensure accountability for AI systems. Organizations should have mechanisms for oversight, compliance with regulations, and addressing the potential social, economic, and ethical implications of AI. Ethical review boards, industry standards, and regulatory frameworks can help guide responsible AI development and deployment.

Safety and Reliability:

AI systems that interact with physical or human environments must prioritize safety. Autonomous vehicles, robotics, and healthcare AI systems, for example, should be designed to minimize risks and avoid harm. Rigorous testing, validation, and continuous monitoring are necessary to ensure the reliability and safety of AI technologies.

Job Displacement and Socioeconomic Impact:

Automation driven by AI can lead to job displacement and socioeconomic shifts. It is crucial to address the impact on workers and communities affected by AI-driven changes. Reskilling programs, education initiatives, and social support systems can help workers transition to new roles and mitigate negative impacts on employment and income inequality.

Human Autonomy and Control:

AI should augment human capabilities rather than replace them. It is essential to maintain human control and decision-making over AI systems. Humans should have the ability to understand, challenge, and override AI decisions, particularly in critical domains like healthcare, criminal justice, and national security.

Environmental Impact:

The environmental impact of AI, including energy consumption and carbon footprint, should be considered. Developing energy-efficient algorithms, optimizing hardware infrastructure, and promoting sustainable practices in AI development and deployment can contribute to mitigating the environmental impact of AI technologies.

Ethical AI Research and Development:

Promoting ethical AI research and development practices is crucial. Ethical considerations should be integrated into the entire AI lifecycle, from data collection and algorithm design to deployment and ongoing monitoring. Encouraging interdisciplinary collaboration, diversity in AI development teams, and ethical guidelines can foster responsible AI innovation.

Public Engagement and Inclusion:

Engaging the public, including affected communities, in AI development and deployment is essential. Inclusive and participatory approaches allow diverse perspectives to be heard, promote fairness, and prevent the concentration of power. Engaging stakeholders, incorporating feedback, and addressing public concerns can lead to more ethically grounded AI systems.

Addressing these ethical challenges presents opportunities to build trust, foster innovation, and ensure AI technologies are developed and deployed for the benefit of society. Ethical considerations should be integrated into AI governance frameworks, organizational practices, and regulatory frameworks to guide responsible AI development and usage. Striking a balance between innovation and ethical principles will pave the way for the responsible and beneficial application of AI technologies.

CHAPTER 9

Resources and Further Learning

9.1 Books, Blogs, and Websites

Here are some recommended books, blogs, and websites to further explore the topic of AI:

Books:

1. "Artificial Intelligence: A Modern Approach" by Stuart Russell and Peter Norvig
2. "Superintelligence: Paths, Dangers, Strategies" by Nick Bostrom
3. "The Master Algorithm: How the Quest for the Ultimate Learning Machine Will Remake Our World" by Pedro Domingos
4. "Human Compatible: Artificial Intelligence and the Problem of Control" by Stuart Russell
5. "Life 3.0: Being Human in the Age of Artificial Intelligence" by Max Tegmark
6. "The Hundred-Page Machine Learning Book" by Andriy Burkov
7. "Deep Learning" by Ian Goodfellow, Yoshua Bengio, and Aaron Courville
8. "Weapons of Math Destruction: How Big Data Increases Inequality and Threatens Democracy" by Cathy O'Neil
9. "Prediction Machines: The Simple Economics of Artificial Intelligence" by Ajay Agrawal, Joshua Gans, and Avi Goldfarb
10. "The AI Book: The Artificial Intelligence Handbook for Business Leaders" by Susanne Chishti and Ivana Bartoletti

Blogs:

1. AI Trends (www.aitrends.com)
2. Towards Data Science (towardsdatascience.com)
3. AI Alignment (www.alignmentforum.org)
4. OpenAI Blog (openai.com/blog)
5. Google AI Blog (ai.googleblog.com)
6. Microsoft AI Blog (blogs.microsoft.com/ai)
7. DeepMind Blog (deepmind.com/blog)
8. The Gradient (thegradient.pub)
9. AI Business (www.ai-business.com)
10. AI Ethics (aiethics.com)

Websites:

1. AI Depot (www.aidepot.com)
2. AI for Everyone (www.ai4everyone.org)
3. AI in Education (aiineducation.org)
4. AI Now Institute (ainowinstitute.org)
5. Future of Life Institute (futureoflife.org)
6. Partnership on AI (www.partnershiponai.org)
7. OpenAI (www.openai.com)
8. IBM Watson (www.ibm.com/watson)
9. NVIDIA AI (www.nvidia.com/en-us/ai)
10. MIT Technology Review - Artificial Intelligence (www.technologyreview.com/ai)

These resources provide a wealth of information, insights, and discussions on various aspects of AI, including its applications, ethics, and implications. They cater to different levels of expertise, from beginners to advanced readers, and offer diverse perspectives from industry experts and researchers. Remember to always critically evaluate the information you encounter and stay updated on the latest developments in the field.

9.2 Online Courses and Tutorials

Here are some online courses and tutorials that can help you further your understanding of AI:

1. Coursera - "AI for Everyone" by deeplearning.ai: This course provides a non-technical introduction to AI concepts, applications, and implications, suitable for beginners and business professionals.
2. Coursera - "Machine Learning" by Andrew Ng: This popular course covers the fundamentals of machine learning, including supervised learning, unsupervised learning, and deep learning.
3. Udacity - "Intro to Artificial Intelligence" by Sebastian Thrun and Peter Norvig: This course offers a comprehensive introduction to AI, covering topics such as search algorithms, game playing, and probabilistic inference.
4. edX - "Deep Learning" by deeplearning.ai: Taught by Andrew Ng, this course delves into the concepts and techniques of deep learning, including neural networks, convolutional networks, and recurrent networks.
5. edX - "Artificial Intelligence" by Columbia University: This course provides a broad overview of AI, including machine learning, natural language processing, and robotics.
6. Stanford University - "CS231n: Convolutional Neural Networks for Visual Recognition": This popular course focuses on deep learning techniques applied to computer vision tasks and is available as free lectures and course materials online.
7. MIT OpenCourseWare - "Artificial Intelligence": This course provides an in-depth exploration of AI topics, including machine learning, perception, reasoning, and language understanding.
8. Kaggle: Kaggle offers a platform for learning and practicing data science and machine learning. It provides tutorials, competitions, and datasets to work on real-world AI problems.
9. TensorFlow Tutorials: TensorFlow, an open-source AI library, offers a collection of tutorials and guides that cover various AI topics, including deep learning, natural language processing, and computer vision.
10. PyTorch Tutorials: PyTorch, another popular deep learning framework, provides tutorials and examples to help you understand and implement AI algorithms using PyTorch.

These courses and tutorials cater to different levels of expertise and provide hands-on learning experiences with real-world applications. Some platforms offer free access to course materials, while others may require a subscription or fee for certification. Choose courses that align with your interests and learning objectives to gain practical skills and knowledge in AI.

9.3 AI Development Tools and Frameworks

There are several popular AI development tools and frameworks that can help you build AI applications and models. Here are some widely used ones:

1. TensorFlow: Developed by Google's Brain Team, TensorFlow is a widely adopted open-source framework for building and training machine learning models. It provides a flexible architecture and supports a range of neural network architectures, including deep learning models.
2. PyTorch: PyTorch is an open-source deep learning framework developed by Facebook's AI Research lab. It is known for its dynamic computation graph and ease of use, making it popular among researchers and developers. PyTorch provides extensive support for neural networks and deep learning algorithms.
3. Keras: Keras is a user-friendly, high-level deep learning library that runs on top of TensorFlow or other backend frameworks. It simplifies the process of building neural networks and allows for rapid prototyping and experimentation.
4. Scikit-learn: Scikit-learn is a popular Python library for machine learning. It provides a wide range of algorithms for tasks such as classification, regression, clustering, and dimensionality reduction. Scikit-learn also offers tools for data preprocessing and model evaluation.
5. Caffe: Caffe is a deep learning framework primarily used for computer vision tasks. It is known for its speed and efficiency, making it suitable for large-scale neural network deployments. Caffe has a strong community and supports a variety of pre-trained models.
6. Theano: Theano is a Python library that allows for efficient mathematical computations, including deep learning operations. It provides a symbolic expression framework for defining and

optimizing mathematical expressions, particularly useful for deep learning models.

7. Microsoft Cognitive Toolkit (CNTK): CNTK is a deep learning framework developed by Microsoft. It offers a scalable and efficient platform for building deep neural networks. CNTK supports distributed training across multiple GPUs and provides a range of neural network building blocks.

8. OpenAI Gym: OpenAI Gym is a toolkit for developing and comparing reinforcement learning algorithms. It provides a wide range of environments and benchmark problems to test and evaluate reinfocement learning models.

9. Apache MXNet: MXNet is a flexible and efficient deep learning framework that supports both imperative and symbolic programming models. It is designed for scalability and allows for distributed training across multiple devices.

10. H2O.ai: H2O.ai is an open-source machine learning platform that provides a user-friendly interface for building and deploying AI models. It supports a wide range of algorithms and offers features for automatic model selection and hyperparameter tuning.

These tools and frameworks provide a variety of options for building AI models and applications, ranging from deep learning to machine learning and reinforcement learning. Choose the one that best fits your requirements, programming language preference, and level of expertise. Many of these frameworks have extensive documentation, tutorials, and online communities that can help you get started and provide support along the way.

9.4 AI Communities and Forums

Engaging with AI communities and forums is a great way to connect with like-minded individuals, stay updated on the latest advancements, and seek guidance on AI-related topics. Here are some popular AI communities and forums you can explore:

1. Reddit - r/MachineLearning: A subreddit dedicated to machine learning, where you can find discussions, news, research papers, and resources related to AI and ML.

2. AI Stack Exchange: A question-and-answer platform specifically focused on artificial intelligence. You can ask questions, seek advice, and participate in discussions on various AI-related topics.
3. Kaggle Forums: Kaggle hosts a vibrant community of data scientists and machine learning practitioners. The forums allow you to collaborate, discuss challenges, share insights, and participate in competitions.
4. Data Science Stack Exchange: A platform for questions and answers on data science topics, including AI and machine learning. It covers a wide range of topics related to AI, data analysis, and predictive modeling.
5. AI Village by OpenAI: An online community created by OpenAI that aims to foster collaboration and discussion on AI-related topics. It includes forums, events, and resources to support AI enthusiasts and practitioners.
6. AI Alignment Forum: A forum dedicated to discussing the alignment of AI systems with human values. It covers topics related to AI safety, ethics, and the long-term implications of AI development.
7. AI for Good Community by the United Nations: An online platform that brings together individuals and organizations working on AI applications for social good. It provides a space for collaboration, knowledge sharing, and discussions on leveraging AI for positive impact.
8. Towards Data Science Community: A community of data scientists, AI practitioners, and enthusiasts. It features articles, tutorials, and discussions on AI, machine learning, and data science topics.
9. AI Ethics Global Village: An online community focused on AI ethics and responsible AI development. It hosts discussions, resources, and events to promote ethical considerations in AI.
10. AI Forums on popular developer platforms: Platforms like GitHub, Stack Overflow, and Dev.to host AI-related forums where developers and AI practitioners can engage in discussions, seek help, and share knowledge.

Engaging with these communities and forums can provide valuable insights, networking opportunities, and access to a diverse range of perspectives in the AI field. Remember to be respectful, contribute positively, and follow community guidelines when participating in discussions.

Conclusion

In conclusion, Artificial Intelligence (AI) is a rapidly evolving field with tremendous potential to transform various aspects of our lives. This beginner's guide to AI has provided an overview of the fundamental concepts, history, real-world applications, and ethical considerations surrounding AI.

We explored the difference between Narrow AI and General AI, as well as key AI techniques such as Machine Learning, Deep Learning, and Reinforcement Learning. We discussed the crucial role of data in fueling AI systems and the importance of algorithms, models, training, and evaluation in AI development.

The guide also covered different types of learning, including Supervised, Unsupervised, and Semi-Supervised Learning, along with the concept of Feature Engineering and evaluation metrics. We then delved into specific AI architectures like Neural Networks, Convolutional Neural Networks (CNNs), Recurrent Neural Networks (RNNs), Transfer Learning, and other common deep learning architectures.

Furthermore, we explored the AI's impact on various industries, including Healthcare, Transportation, Education, and Business, discussing the opportunities and challenges that arise. We also highlighted the ethical considerations surrounding AI, such as bias, privacy, transparency, accountability, and governance.

To further expand your knowledge, we recommended books, blogs, and websites that cover AI in depth. Additionally, we suggested online courses and tutorials that provide hands-on learning experiences. Lastly, we mentioned AI development tools and frameworks that can assist in building AI applications and models, as well as AI communities and forums for engagement and collaboration.

As AI continues to advance, it is essential to stay informed, actively participate in discussions, and approach AI development and deployment with ethical considerations in mind. By embracing responsible AI practices, we can harness the potential of AI to create a positive and inclusive impact on society.

Remember, this beginner's guide provides a foundation, but AI is a vast and ever-evolving field. Continuously exploring, learning, and adapting to new developments is key to staying abreast of the latest advancements and discoveries in AI.

www.ingramcontent.com/pod-product-compliance
Lightning Source LLC
LaVergne TN
LVHW051658050326

832903LV00032B/3893